Wonders
of the
Catholic Faith

Fr. Francisco Radecki, CMRI

ISBN Number: 978-0-9882744-3-3

Library of Congress Control Number: 2015904126

Printed by Bookmasters, Inc.   Ashland, Ohio

St. Joseph's Media

P. O. Box 186	P.O. Box 220208
Wayne, Michigan	Newhall, California
48184-0186	91322

stjosephsmedia.com

Dedicated to two champions of the Catholic Faith

Bishop Mark Pivarunas, CMRI

and

Father Dominic Radecki, CMRI

Acknowledgements

Wonders of the Catholic Faith took over two years to complete. It is a combination of sermon notes of Fr. Francisco Radecki, CMRI typed by Paula Storm and contributions from students of his Theology Class at St. Joseph's Catholic School in Wayne, Michigan: Megan and Michelle Tibai and Ryan and William Sentman.

Special thanks to my twin, Fr. Dominic Radecki, CMRI, Fr. Gregory Drahman, CMRI, and Fr. Gabriel Lavery, CMRI for their theological editing and to Linda Chomin and Gwen Dietrich for their editorial assistance.

Special thanks to Amanda Diehl for her inspiring cover design and to school faculty members Sr. Mary Petra, CMRI; Sr. Marie Janae, CMRI; Sr. Corinne Marie, CMRI, Harutun Karian, PhD; Paula Storm, AA, BA, MILS, and Esther Hanadel for their advice and practical comments.

The students came to better understand and appreciate their Catholic Faith as they helped write this book. Notes from the book helped instruct several converts.

Table of Contents

Introduction

The Catholic Faith, a treasure that Jesus Christ entrusted to His Church, has inspired and guided millions through the centuries. The Catholic Church remains today as a lighthouse to guide souls to God and to lead them to eternal salvation.

It is truly remarkable how Our Lord's teachings cover so many areas yet remain concise, easy to understand and unchanged for nearly 2,000 years. This shows the Catholic Faith is not something that has to be intimidating nor very complex.

Wonders of the Catholic Faith presents Catholic doctrines in a very readable, enjoyable style. Stories illustrate and reinforce the lessons and give logical refutations of modern errors. This book is a manual, reference book, textbook, and devotional work all in one.

Instead of using a typical question and answer format, this catechism draws inspiration from Sacred Scripture, Apostolic Tradition, the writings of the Popes, the Saints, the Fathers and Doctors of the Church, the *Baltimore Catechism,* and the *Catechism of the Council of Trent.*

Wonders of the Catholic Faith gives a logical foundation for essential Catholic beliefs and the reasons for its various practices. It answers questions and confirms the faith of even Cradle Catholics. Clergy can use this book for sermon outlines, to assist those interested in joining the Church, as well as to instruct those curious about the Faith. Important facts are given in bold or italic type to help students.

Questions for each chapter make it an interactive book, excellent for use in homeschool theology classes, high school classrooms, and adult catechism study.

I suggest that you also read Fr. Francisco Radecki's book *The Family Catechism* for additional information. Its' 100 color illustrations, prayers and lessons further elucidate Catholic belief and practices.

Wonders of the Catholic Faith is a practical guide for Catholics today. It not only explains the teachings of the Church, but also shows how to get to Heaven. After all, this is the ultimate purpose of Christ founding the Catholic Church. This book will fortify the faith of Catholics, educate potential converts and inspire all who are seeking the truth.

Paula M. Storm, AA, BA, MILS
Associate Professor, Eastern Michigan University

Wonders of the Catholic Faith

For many Cradle Catholics, Christ's teachings have become a way of life. The various mysteries, dogmas, commandments, laws, liturgical seasons, and feasts are viewed as one entity.

Our Lord, in establishing the Catholic Church, did not intend it to be merely another institution. His aim was to use the Church and the Catholic Faith as the means of transforming sinners into saints, leading souls from earth to Heaven and assisting His adopted children in the transition from time to eternity.

Enlightened by faith, encouraged by hope and animated by charity, Jesus' true followers strive to imitate His virtues and be enkindled with His love. Strengthened by grace, they keep the commandments and become a source of inspiration to all.

Prayer touches every aspect of a Catholic's life and is woven into each chapter of this book. Prayer is one of the most important actions of each day.

The reverent liturgy, life-giving sacraments, elevated teachings, and Church's hierarchical structure manifest the divine. This explains how one religion can be perfectly adapted to all times, regions, peoples, and tongues, yet remain uniform and retain doctrinal and liturgical integrity.

One must marvel at the wondrous vitality of the Catholic Church that has survived twenty-one centuries of persecution, attacks by heretics, schismatics, apostates, antipopes, false councils, and the very legions of Hell. In spite of all, it will last until the end of time and remain as a beacon—enlightening and guiding souls on their journey to their heavenly home.

My prayer is that this book will animate your faith, increase your confidence in God and help you love God deeply, and your neighbor as yourself.

Fr. Francisco Radecki, CMRI

Chapter One

Proofs for the Existence of God

Intelligent Design / Almighty Power

The world in which we live manifests countless wonders that are beyond human capability. They could not have occurred by chance or randomly evolved by themselves, but are the result of infinite intelligence and power. The world could only have been created, preserved and maintained by a Supreme Being, Almighty God.

St. Thomas Aquinas (1225-1274) proved the existence of an all-powerful, all-good God and demonstrated His divine wisdom and providential care over the world and human beings.

First Cause

Since nature works for a determinate end under the direction of a higher agent, whatever is done by nature must needs be traced back to God, as to its first cause.[1] ...Now whatever lacks intelligence cannot move toward an end, unless it be directed by some being endowed with knowledge and intelligence; as the arrow is shot to its mark by an archer. Therefore, some Intelligent Being exists by whom all natural things are directed to their end; and this Being we call God.[2] In the beginning, God created Heaven and earth.[3]

Cause and Effect

The human body and the smallest insect encompass such perfection that it is impossible for them to have been the work of chance. The vast array of life forms from microscopic organisms to the blue whale resemble an orchestra in harmony and demonstrate the work of a supremely intelligent Master Planner. For every effect there must be a cause.

Some evolutionists believe matter is eternal. Since it is not the result of human effort, where did it come from? Every effect needs a cause. Material things must have a starting point.

Order

No human being possesses the unlimited power and wisdom necessary to preserve and maintain the universe, nor to make the sun rise and set daily. Who established the laws of physics and set them in motion in the first place? No one can rationally say this incredible world evolved by itself or was the result of a random "big bang." The universe is too perfectly ordered to have been the result of an accident, random explosion or chemical reaction.

If the world was formed without an Intelligent Designer or merely evolved as a result of natural selection, how do certain fish, animals and insects develop camouflage? The fact that every snowflake is unique and that leaves turn exquisite colors as they fall from trees and die are proofs of design and order in the world. Who created them that way?

There is an undeniable order in nature that points to a Being with supreme intelligence Who reveals Himself through His creation. The progression of seasons, the cycles of night and day, the orbits of the planets, the perfect balance between prey and predator, vegetative and animate life point to an all-powerful Creator—Almighty God.

---

[1] St. Thomas Aquinas, *Summa Theologica,* Q. 2, Art. 3, p. 14 (English Translation).
[2] Aquinas, Reply to Obj. 2, 14.
[3] Genesis 1, 1.

Order throughout the universe, relegating each creature and inanimate object to fulfill a common purpose, points to an infinitely intelligent Supreme Being. Intelligent design and harmonious order are pre-determined, not achieved by accident.

Law

All human societies need laws. Without law, anarchy would be rampant. Just laws are intended to ensure the common good of society and individuals.

People naturally do not like their liberty restricted by laws. Therefore, law must have its origin from an ultimate Law Giver, Almighty God. The Ten Commandments (also known as Natural Law) are written in the heart of every individual.[4] It is not enough to merely know the law. St. Paul wrote: "...It is they who follow the law that will be justified."[5]

Conscience

Persons, having attained the use of reason and with no mental disability, naturally know they are accountable for their actions and certain activities are right and others intrinsically wrong. Catechisms define conscience as a judgment of right reason that reminds individuals of their obligations to God and neighbor, and warns them of the consequences of sinful actions. The Confraternity of Christian Doctrine simplified this scholastic definition:

> There is a voice in his heart that makes him feel responsible for his deliberate actions to someone else. ...He recognizes it without saying it that there is a law imposed by Someone greater than himself. That Someone is God.[6]

Cardinal Newman taught that people understand they are personally responsible for their actions and are often ashamed and frightened when transgressing the voice of conscience.[7] Although people can tragically silence their conscience through repeated evil acts, they are still responsible for them. Fr. Conway in *The Question Box* says:

> Conscience speaks of a necessary duty we owe. It brings us face to face with an obligatory law, whose commands are authoritative, and whose dictates are final, and unquestioned.[8]

God is All-Just

Some believe that because God is all-merciful, everyone will go to Heaven. They forget that God is also all-just and what a person sows, he reaps. Scripture describes both attributes of God: "For mercy and wrath are with Him. He is mighty to forgive, and to pour out indignation."[9] Heaven is not something automatically given to all. It is a reward for keeping the Ten Commandments and for leading a virtuous life.

Jesus Christ said, "Not everyone who says to Me, 'Lord, Lord,' shall enter the kingdom of Heaven; but he who does the will of My Father in Heaven shall enter the kingdom of Heaven."[10] The good deserve to be rewarded and the wicked to be punished. Societies have prisons to penalize criminals who break laws; therefore, in justice God likewise must punish sinners who disregard His commandments.

---

[4] See Romans 2, 15.
[5] Romans 2, 13.
[6] *Catholic Doctrine First Semester*, p. 10.
[7] See *Grammar of Assent*, p. 109.
[8] p. 3.
[9] Ecclesiasticus 16, 12.
[10] Matthew 7, 21.

Chapter Two

Atheistic Evolution / The Big Bang Theory

Atheists and non-believers promote atheistic evolution in order to explain the existence of the world without reference to God, as if living things could automatically appear, evolve from one another, and sprout wings or grow legs as needed.

Natural laws of genus and species prove living things don't mutate into other forms. Mummified cats and crocodiles are replicas of current ones and ancient insects identical to many of those seen today.

Even though Charles Darwin is widely recognized as the father of evolution, French scientist Pierre Simon Laplace (1749-1827) helped expel God from science.

> Laplace wrote a book on astronomy, which didn't mention God. And when Napoleon asked him why God isn't mentioned, Laplace famously replied, 'Sire, I had no need of that hypothesis.'[11]

Atheists at Work

During the eighteenth, nineteenth and twentieth centuries, atheists, agnostics and the financiers who supported them, encouraged philosophers and scientists to teach the masses from a naturalistic point of view. They eliminated references to the supernatural in order to deny the existence of God Who loves each individual and created and preserves the world.

The vacuum cast them into the spotlight as learned scholars and fearless pioneers in the field of science. Many as a result earned worldwide popularity.

Darwinian Evolution

The theory of evolution of British geologist and naturalist Charles Darwin (1809-1882) removes God from creation and maintains that the world had no plan or design but was merely the result of random forces and the survival of the fittest.

Darwin's concept of *natural selection* claims that living organisms spontaneously adapt to their environment. His *theory of evolution* taught that creatures randomly and naturally evolve into others.

By including man in this process, saying that humans evolved from apes, Darwin reduced them to the status of mere animals. He never explained how the first cell was formed, how the ape/man developed intellect and reason, how superior things emerged from inferior, or why the evolutionary trend does not continue today.

Although evolution is merely a hypothesis, it is revered as a law today. A skeptic, who did not believe in God, invented this irrational theory. It has never been, nor will it ever be proven. Scientific method demands that any hypothesis be either proven or disproven by experimentation. Otherwise, it can never become a law.

Persons who don't believe in God are often willing to believe anything. Physical chemist, Harutun Karian, PhD claims those who espouse atheistic evolution believe that creation occurred randomly—like a deck of cards being throw haphazardly into the air and then landing in perfect descending order.

---

[11] Ian Markham, *Against Atheism: Why Dawkins, Hitchens, and Harris Are Fundamentally Wrong*, p. 65.

Ramifications of Evolution

Darwin appeared at a time when naturalism and humanism permeated society. He helped transform the life sciences from a God-centered to a materialistic point of view and his ideas quickly spread from the natural sciences to other disciplines.

Fredrick Nietzche (1844-1900) based a number of his atheistic, philosophical concepts on Darwin's beliefs. These also profoundly influenced Sigmund Freud's (1856-1939) theories in the field of psychiatry.

Marx and Engels adopted Darwin's hypothesis to view people as dispensable. This allows Communists to systematically eliminate undesirables. Scholars, world leaders and industrialists tried to justify the practice of exploiting citizens, workers and the use of child labor by applying the theories of Herbert Spencer, originator of Social Darwinism.

This paradigm shift has caused ramifications in every facet of society. If human beings are mere animals, they can be utilized or eliminated as conditions dictate.

By turning society away from God, atheistic evolution is responsible for many of society's ills including abortion, euthanasia, human trafficking, and genocide. Hitler, Stalin, Mao Zedong, Pol Pot, Idi Amin, and drug lords justified inhumane cruelty and treated people like animals.

The Second Law of Thermodynamics

Science and religion are not in conflict. God established the laws of nature, which describe the behavior of matter and energy in order to preserve order in nature. God created matter out of nothing and established the laws of physics. Einstein showed the close relationship between matter and energy by his famous equation of $E=mc^2$. Consequently, the sciences of chemistry and physics dictate that matter and energy are conserved so that it is not possible to create or destroy either form of existence.

From a theological point of view, this means that once God completed creation, He stopped the creative process so that no further generation of matter and energy occurred. This applies to all space and time so there is no room for evolution to occur. The time that evolutionists bank on is not available to alter God's plan in creation.

The Second Law of Thermodynamics basically indicates that there is a tendency for all matter to become disordered with the progression of time. The possibility of disorganized matter to reassemble into an ordered existence is beyond the laws of thermodynamics.

Even Albert Einstein in 1905 declared that if there was any physical law that resists any change in the future, it is the law of thermodynamics. Although evolution is based on the need for a vast expanse of time it has no scientific justification.

Darwin, who denied a Creator, held that matter had a mind of its own. Einstein, on the contrary said, "God does not play dice."

> Metal rusts, it does not unrust. Milk spills, it does not unspill. China cups break, they do not unbreak. In general, things age; they wear out; they decay. Rocks erode, paper grows yellow and crumbles, clothing becomes threadbare, memories fade. Nothing withstands 'the ravages of time.'[12]

[12] Stephen Barr, *Modern Physics and Ancient Faith*, p. 60.

Regarding chemical changes, (like the formation of rust by the combination of oxygen and iron), iron oxide cannot revert to the elements of oxygen and iron by itself. Through the application of heat, the original elements will be generated, but this is creating more disorder, not establishing order as evolution teaches.

The formation of rust resembles the decay of a dead object. To claim that a living organism can be formed from a decayed substance is like believing rust can transform itself into iron and then reassemble into a mighty battleship.

Church Teaching

The Fourth Lateran Council and the Vatican Council of 1869-1870 taught as a dogma of faith[13] that God created the world out of nothing.[14] "God alone is the immediate efficient cause of creation. This is *de fide* from the Ordinary Magisterium of the Church."[15] In his encyclical *Humani Generis* of August 12, 1950, Pope Pius XII condemned atheistic evolution and wrote that the scriptural account of creation is immune from error and divinely inspired.

> ...Catholic Faith obliges us to hold that souls are immediately created by God. ...the first eleven books of Genesis... pertain to history... give a popular description of the origin of the human race...

The Big Bang Theory

Belgian priest / physicist Fr. Georges Lemaître (1894-1966) invented the Big Bang Theory. Previously, nonbelievers explained the world around them by transmutation of species, Darwin's evolution or the belief the universe had always existed.

The Big Bang Theory claims that a gigantic explosion caused by a concentrated atom formed the universe. The resultant intense heat caused chaotic expanding waves that produced matter, stars, planets, heavenly bodies, galaxies, the sun, and the Earth. Atheists hold that this was a chaotic, random act. Theists believe this was an act of God, well orchestrated and engineered by Him.

Since God has infinite power He could have created the world in an instant. In an address to the Pontifical Academy of Science in 1951 Pope Pius XII referred to creation as being an ordered act. It is unreasonable to believe a random Big Bang devoid of divine intervention formed the universe and this cannot be reconciled with Genesis nor Pope Pius XII.

Real World Examples

There is no evidence that the universe was created by accident. During an explosion, matter is usually deformed and destroyed. Two massive fireballs appear when a projectile is shot from an American M1 Abrams battle tank—one at the muzzle and one at the point of entry. Fireworks, on the other hand, are ordered and beautiful. They involve design and a precise knowledge of materials and their reaction at ignition and are not the result of random forces.

Another Option

Sir Isaac Newton (1642-1727) wrote, "This most beautiful system [the Universe] could only proceed from the counsel and dominion of an intelligent Being."[16] Lord Kelvin (1824-1907) said, "Nature declares that there is one ever-acting Creator and Ruler."[17]

---

[13] That Catholics must believe (*de fide*).
[14] See Very Rev. Adolfe Tanquerey, SS, DD, *Manual of Dogmatic Theology: Volume One,* p. 360.
[15] Tanquerey, 361.
[16] J. Hutchins, *Hubble Reveals Creation By An Awe-Inspiring Power,* cover jacket.
[17] Martin Scott, SJ, LittD, *Things Catholic are Asked About,* p. 251.

Therefore, since God possesses infinite power, He can do whatever He pleases. J. Hutchins reasons that God could have created the world by means of a massive explosion that would resemble a magnificent fireworks display. An ordered, awe-inspiring display of power could have been the means chosen by God to create the world around us.

As man explores the universe with Hubble, Spitzer and other space telescopes, it becomes apparent that there is order in the design of the universe and evidence of a Grand Designer.

...When we see the images delivered to us from space and the variety of galaxies, stars, nebula, quasars, neutron stars, black holes, supernovas, and other cosmic effects, we can only imagine that these creative displays of energy were conceived and prepared by a Superior Craftsman and not just some random event.[18]

Opinions of Renowned Scientists

Vera Kistiakowsky   *MIT physicist*

The exquisite order displayed by our scientific understanding of the physical world calls for the divine.

George Ellis   *British astrophysicist*

Amazing fine tuning occurs in the laws that make this [complexity] possible. Realization of the complexity of what is accomplished makes it very difficult not to use the word 'miraculous'...

Henry Schaefer   *Professor of Chemistry at the University of Georgia*

The significance and joy in my science comes in those occasional moments of discovering something new and saying to myself, 'So that's how God did it.' My goal is to understand a little corner of God's plan.

Paul Davies   *British Astrophysicist*

There is for me powerful evidence that there is something going on behind it all... The impression of design is overwhelming. The laws [of physics]... seem to be the product of exceedingly ingenious design...

George Greenstein   *Astronomer*

As we survey all the evidence, the thought insistently arises that some supernatural agency - or, rather, Agency - must be involved. Is it possible that suddenly, without intending to, we have stumbled upon scientific proof of the existence of a Supreme Being?

Robert Jastrow   *Self-proclaimed agnostic*

For the scientist who has lived by his faith in the power of reason, the story ends like a bad dream. He has scaled the mountains of ignorance; he is about to conquer the highest peak; as he pulls himself over the final rock, he is greeted by a band of theologians who have been sitting there for centuries.

Arthur Schawlow   *Professor of Physics at Stanford University, 1981 Nobel Prize in physics*

It seems to me that when confronted with the marvels of life and the universe, one must ask why and not just how. The only possible answers are religious. ...I find a need for God in the universe and in my own life.

Wernher von Braun   *NASA Rocket engineer*

I find it as difficult to understand a scientist who does not acknowledge the presence of a superior rationality behind the existence of the universe as it is to comprehend a theologian who would deny the advances of science.[19]

---

[18] *Hubble Reveals Creation By An Awe-Inspiring Power,* p. 47.
[19] Passages taken from Rich Deem's *Quotes from Scientists Regarding Design of the Universe.* www.godandscience.org/apologetics/quotes.html#n02

Chapter Three
The Blessed Trinity

The *Baltimore Catechism* defines God as "the Supreme Being, infinitely perfect, who made all things and keeps them in existence."[20] He is almighty, eternal, immutable, all perfect, all just, all knowing, and all merciful. Nothing escapes His knowledge. His perfections and power are infinite. God will reward or punish every individual according to a person's merits or sins, based on one's observance of the Ten Commandments.

There are Three Divine Persons in One God—Father, Son and Holy Ghost. The doctrine of the Blessed Trinity (Three Divine Persons in one Divine Nature—the Triune God) is a supernatural mystery that cannot be completely comprehended in this life.

The mystery of the Blessed Trinity is beyond human reason, not contrary to it. Two created things that help individuals better understand this mystery are the triangle and the shamrock, a three-leaf clover.

Catholics Profess their Belief in the Blessed Trinity in Numerous Ways

- The *Sign of the Cross* and *Apostles Creed* are believed to date back to Apostolic Times
- The prayer: *Glory be to the Father and to the Son and to the Holy Ghost as it was in the beginning is now and ever shall be world without end. Amen.*
- Mass Prayers: *Gloria, Nicene Creed, Trinity Preface, Suscipe Sancta Trinitas,* and *Placeat*

The Blessed Trinity

God had no beginning and existed from eternity. God the Father is unbegotten. Jesus Christ, the only begotten Son of the Father has two distinct natures—the divine nature of God and the human nature of man (body and soul). God the Holy Ghost proceeds from the love of the Father and the Son. St. Thomas Aquinas in his work *De Doctrina Christiana* simply says that the "Trinity is one God from Whom, through Whom and in Whom all things exist."

Scripture attributes different activities to each of the Three Divine Persons. Even though They are distinct, They act in unison. St. Augustine explains:

> The Church is accustomed most fittingly to attribute to the Father those works of the divinity in which power excels, to the Son those in which wisdom excels and to the Holy Ghost those in which love excels. Not that all perfections and external operations of the Trinity are not common to the Divine Person; for the operations of the Trinity are indivisible, even as the essence of the Trinity is indivisible.[21]

Old Testament References

The mystery of the Blessed Trinity wasn't revealed to the Chosen People since they were prone to idolatry and may have tried to worship multiple gods. The Old Testament refers to God as "I am Who am"[22] and the God of Abraham, the God of Isaac and the God of Jacob. Genesis says "Let Us make man to our image and likeness"[23] and "Let Us go down, and there confound their tongue, [at the Tower of Babel] that they may not understand one another's speech."[24]

---

[20] p. 5.
[21] Matthew 3, 16-17.
[22] Exodus 3, 14.
[23] Chapter 1, Verse 26.
[24] Chapter 11, Verse 7.

New Testament References

Christ commanded the Apostles and their successors to baptize in the name of the Father and of the Son and of the Holy Ghost.[25] Our Lord demonstrated the relationship between the Three Divine Persons when He referred to the Holy Ghost "whom I will send from the Father."[26]

All Three Divine Persons were manifested during the Baptism of Jesus in the River Jordan.

> And behold, the heavens were opened to him [St. John the Baptist], and he saw the Spirit of God descending as a dove and coming upon Him [Jesus]. And behold, a voice from the heavens said, 'This is My Beloved Son, in whom I am well pleased.'[27]

Fr. Tanquerey notes that *"it is evident that,* therefore, that *those three* are not one person, *but three persons really distinct,"* yet the Father, and the Son and the Holy Ghost "are united by *one* and the *same* [divine] *nature."*[28]

Obligations to God

"The primary end of creatures is the manifesting and glorifying of God's goodness; the secondary end is the good of creatures."[29] Since God created every human, each person has an obligation to know, love and serve Him on earth. In return, God will reward those individuals with the perfect happiness of Heaven. Those who reject God and His laws will be justly punished. Pope Pius XI wrote: "Belief in God is the unshaken foundation of all social order and of all responsible action on earth."[30]

A person can only know God and His teachings through the one, true religion He established, the Catholic Church. An individual's knowledge of God is deepened by instruction in the Faith, sermons and books on Catholic belief, learning more about the Bible and Tradition, and viewing the world He created which reflects His goodness and power. A person thereby comes to a better realization of God's wondrous works and of the relationship that exists between Him and humans through creation, redemption and sanctification.

Knowledge of God's goodness leads one to love and serve Him by faithfully keeping His laws—the Ten Commandments, praying to Him, attending Sunday Mass, and leading a virtuous life. God expects Catholics to be a light to the world and to edify others by the practice of their faith. This glorifies God, inspires others and causes many that have drifted to return to God.

Accountability

Reason demands that good actions be rewarded and evil ones punished. Since perfect justice is not possible in this life, it must be attained in the next. On earth, it frequently happens that good people suffer and struggle while the wicked prosper and lead relatively carefree lives.

During the *Particular Judgment* at the moment of death, Jesus judges each individual at the place where the person died and determines where he or she will spend eternity. At the *General Judgment* at the End of the World all will acknowledge the justice of God. There the good will be vindicated and the evil condemned.

---

[25] Matthew 28, 19.
[26] John 16, 26.
[27] Matthew 3, 16-17.
[28] *Manual of Dogmatic Theology: Volume One,* p. 319.
[29] Tanquerey, 363.
[30] *Caritate Christi,* May 3, 1932.

Chapter Four
Erroneous Concepts of God

God is the Almighty Creator, Lord of Heaven and Earth, the First Cause Who is Himself uncaused. He is above all of His creatures and separate from them.

The Blessed Trinity is the one, true God and the Catholic Church the one, true religion established by Jesus Christ. Therefore, the other gods fashioned by people and religions formed through the course of time are false. King David wrote: "For all the gods of the Gentiles are devils, but the Lord made the heavens."[31]

False Concepts of God Today

Many today view God as an indulgent grandfather who sends everyone to Heaven and lets people do whatever they want. Some transform Jesus into merely a holy man from Nazareth. Others see the Holy Ghost as a spiritual force that condones everything.

Agnostics claim that an unknowable God started everything and walked away, like an aloof mad scientist. This ideology of perpetual doubt allows people to live a materialistic, sinful life and justifies ignoring God and His laws.

Atheists claim there is no God. Even though they realize in their hearts that there is a God, they don't want to obey Him and be accountable for their actions. Scripture says, "The fool hath said in his heart: There is no god."[32] It is interesting that no matter how hard people fight to eradicate God from society, He always reappears.

Materialists make the acquisition of material things a false god and the ultimate goal of life. Many are so attached to, and enamored of material possessions and pleasure, they have no time for God and often have no desire for an afterlife of perfect happiness.

Pantheists erroneously claim that the constantly changing material world is divine. Since God is by His very nature, perfect and unchangeable, He cannot be equated with what is limited, mortal and imperfect. Some today embrace pantheism because it theoretically frees them from being accountable to a higher authority and absolves them of moral responsibility.

Unbelievers, also called infidels (those lacking faith) worship idols, nature, creatures, or their rulers. They fail to realize that created, finite things couldn't be God.

Reincarnation

Many pantheists believe that they will be changed into another life form after death. Reincarnation is opposed to both Scripture and reason and there is no proof for this hypothesis. St. Paul condemned the concept when he wrote: "It is appointed unto men to die once and after this comes the judgment."[33]

Reincarnation gives a false hope that one's conduct in this life doesn't matter since after death individuals are given additional chances until they get it right. If there is no judgment, Heaven, Hell, or Purgatory, what motivation is there for one to lead a good life?

---

[31] Psalm 95, 5.
[32] Psalm 13, 1.
[33] Hebrews 9, 27.

Effects of Lack of Faith in God

Life without God is empty and lacks purpose. Those who reject prayer or lack proper guidance often wander aimlessly and never understand the real meaning of life. Those attached to the world often live a life devoid of God and search for happiness but never find it. Many who have never had a relationship with God lose hope once they lose friends, their youthfulness and good health, or find themselves alone without human affection.

God alone gives real meaning to life. He raises those who have fallen, comforts the sorrowful, assists those in need, and offers eternal joy to those who follow His teachings and keep the commandments.

Chapter Five

Unjustly Blaming God for Difficulties

Some people today ask how an all-good God could allow evil in the world. Fr. Pohle writes that God cannot will physical or moral evil for its own sake or as an end in itself.[34] Fr. Conway explains that God permits it "only because in His divine plan they will further either the general good or man's good."[35] St. Augustine teaches that God "...is powerful enough and good enough to make good even out of evil."[36]

Physical evils—The Council of Trent teaches that death, suffering and sickness are a result of original sin.[37] Other physical evils are frequently punishments for sin.

Sin is **moral evil**. "It is an article of the faith that sin can only happen with the permission of God."[38] "For the holiness of God involves an infinite hatred of sin, no matter whether it is considered as an end or a means to an end."[39] Sacred Scripture elucidates this point and describes free will and personal accountability before God for one's actions.

> Before man is life and death, good and evil, that which he shall choose shall be given him:
>
> For the wisdom of God is great, and He is strong in power, seeing all men without ceasing. The eyes of the Lord are towards them that fear Him, and He knoweth all the work of man. He hath commanded no man to do wickedly, and he hath given no man license to sin: for He desireth not a multitude of faithless and unprofitable children.[40]

Drawing Good Out of Evil

St. Augustine says that it is greater for God to draw good out of evil than never to have allowed it in the first place. St. John Chrysostom teaches that God permits the mixture of good and evil, as shown in the parable of the wheat and the cockle, in the hope that sinners convert and save their soul.[41] St. Thomas Aquinas wrote "If all evils were prevented, many good things would be absent from the world."[42] Christ would never have come to earth and God's love would never be as clearly known and understood as it is today.

Apparent Evils

God's permissive will allows evil in order to achieve a greater good. God created the world to follow its natural course—progression of seasons and weather patterns. Although forest fires cause devastation, they germinate new life. Natural disasters cause a number of individuals to pray, focus more on spiritual things and raise their hearts to God. Sadly, others may turn against Him due to anger at the loss of their loved ones or their material possessions.

---

[34] See *God: His Knowability, Essence and Attributes,* p. 443.
[35] *The Question Box,* p. 13.
[36] *Enchiridion Symbolorum,* Chapter XI.
[37] Session V, Canon II.
[38] Rt. Rev. Msgr. Joseph Pohle, PhD, DD. *God: His Knowability, Essence and Attributes,* p. 445. See St. Thomas Aquinas, *Summa Theologica* 1a, q. 19, art. 9 and St. Augustine, *Enchiridion Symbolorum,* c. 46.
[39] Pohle, 443.
[40] Ecclesiasticus 15, 18-21.
[41] See *The Sunday Gospels for Priest and People,* Rev. James Carey, MA, p. 125.
[42] *Summa Theologica* 1, q. 22, art. 2, ad 2.

Suffering

God allows suffering in order to repair for sin and as a punishment for sins committed. When properly accepted, suffering may become a source of great merit. The lives of Our Lord and Our Lady were filled with joy and suffering, as are all lives. Jesus said: "If anyone wishes to come after Me, let him deny himself, and take up his cross and follow Me."[43] He also taught "Unless you do penance you shall all likewise perish."[44]

The Acts of the Apostles says, "through many tribulations we must enter the kingdom of God."[45] St. Cyril of Alexandria reminded his flock of the reward given to those who patiently endure suffering for St. Paul writes, "the sufferings of the present time are not worthy to be compared to the glory to come..."[46]

The earth cannot offer perfect happiness since humans were created for Heaven. Although suffering is naturally repugnant, it can be either a positive or negative part of someone's life. Trials can become a source of merit and purification and a chance to practice resignation, patience, compassion, and faith, hope, and charity in a heroic degree.

Many complain about suffering while others patiently endure it, thereby imitating Christ. Suffering becomes easier when individuals unite their sufferings with those of Jesus.

Some cause their own suffering by making bad choices. For example, alcoholics often develop liver disease; the immoral contract sexually transmitted diseases and AIDS; gamblers incur bankruptcy, and drug abusers loss of memory, heart conditions and death from overdose.

God often allows suffering to bring people back to the observance of the Ten Commandments before they die. As a result, many have returned to God since their suffering led them to view life with eternity in mind.

Financial Problems

God provides the necessities of life for all and is not responsible for paying a person's bills. Some people cause their own problems and then blame God when He doesn't intervene. Some financial difficulties are unavoidable, while others are of one's own making. The fact that life is not perfect makes man long for his true home, Heaven.

God created the world and supplies crops, trees, rain, and the necessities of life for both good and bad alike. "He makes his sun to rise on the good and the evil, and sends rain on the just and the unjust."[47] Some people expect God to immediately grant all their wants and get angry when He doesn't, even though He supplies all their essential needs.

War

The devil often inspires men to instigate wars in order to achieve wealth or power. War is a punishment for sin. Although war causes great hardships, it can also spread culture and customs, allowing individuals and nations to practice mutual charity in the restoration process.

---

[43] Matthew 16, 24.
[44] Luke 13, 3.
[45] Chapter 14, Verse 21.
[46] Romans 8, 18.
[47] Matthew 5, 45.

War may also bring about conversions and encourage people of different nationalities to marry. A Saracen princess helped a captured English knight, who taught her the rudiments of the Catholic Faith, to escape from prison. She later joined him in England, converted and they married. Their son is St. Thomas à Becket.

History has proven that through wars, bloodlines are strengthened. God in His wisdom planned that good characteristics from various nationalities would thereby mingle since isolationism and inbreeding weakens strains.

Illness

Illness is an effect of original sin. Acute illness is a means of merit when properly accepted. God often teaches patience to the sufferer and the caretakers.

Removed from daily routine, sufferers with chronic illness have time to think about God and eternity. Life threatening maladies show the transitory nature of life and give a person time to prepare for death.

Death

Death is an effect of original sin and the means by which all enter eternity. St. Ambrose describes death as the separation of the soul from the body. This teaching is confirmed by the *Catechism of the Council of Trent.*

> ...of the two constituent parts of man, soul and body, one only, that is, the body, is corrupted and returns to its original dust, while the soul remains incorrupt and immortal.[48]

Although attending a funeral is a sobering experience, it puts life in true perspective. The contrast between the mortality of the human body and the immortality of the human soul is in high relief. It is a reminder of the shortness of life on earth and of the eternity that follows. Death was intended to be a peaceful exit from this world, but to those who lead lives of unrepentant sin it becomes a torment, especially with the thought of impending judgment.

Sin

God may tolerate sin for a time so the individual can make a true, lasting conversion, practice a virtuous life and lead others to repentance. Saints repented of their sins and led holy lives. Some well-known penitents include St. Mary Magdalen, St. Augustine and St. Dismas, the good thief.

Jesus Came to Call Sinners to Repentance

Our Lord came to redeem the human-race and to show the way to Heaven. He ate with publicans and sinners so they could be converted and return to God. Jesus Christ said: "It is not the healthy that need a physician, but they who are sick."[49] He told the Pharisees:

> Go and learn what this means. 'I desire mercy and not sacrifice.'[50] I have not come to call the just, but sinners, to repentance.[51]

---

[48] p. 121.
[49] Matthew 9, 12.
[50] Matthew 9, 13.
[51] Luke 5, 32.

"Converts make the best Catholics," describes the fervor of those living the Faith after their conversion. Repentant sinners manifest both the power of God's grace and, the necessity of the will to turn away from sin in order to merit the eternal happiness of Heaven.

Ultimately, a Matter of Faith

Suffering is ultimately a mystery. Even Our Lord during the Agony of the Garden prayed "...Father, if Thou wilt, remove this chalice from Me: but yet not My will, but Thine be done."[52]

No human mind can comprehend God's designs. "For who has known the mind of the Lord or who has been His counselor?"[53] "For as the heavens are exalted above the earth so are My ways exalted above your ways."[54]

Divine Providence

Divine Providence is the name given to God's care over all human beings and the world directing them to their determined end. This is a *de fide* dogma of the Catholic Faith that was defined at the Vatican Council of 1869-1870. "God protects and governs by His Providence all things that He made, reaching from end to end mightily, and ordering all things sweetly."[55]

St. Thomas Aquinas and St. Francis de Sales taught that nothing so enkindles the love of God as the realization of the particular benefits received from Him. God knows the needs of all and provides them, but He also expects each person, in turn, to do his or her part. St. Augustine said God created you without your volition, but will not save you without your effort.[56]

Archbishop Luis Martinez of Mexico City summarized these thoughts when he wrote: "If God loves, me, if He cares for me constantly, if His heart's loving solicitude attends every event of my life, I can and ought to live in peace."[57] St. Paul simply said: "Now we know that to those who love God all things work together unto good...[58]"

---

[52] Luke 22, 42.
[53] Romans 11, 34.
[54] Isaias 55, 9.
[55] Session III, Chapter I, Denzinger-Bannwart, *Enchiridion Symbolorum*, 1784, (1633). See Wisdom 8, 1.
[56] See *Sermo. 15 de Verb. Apost.*, c. 11, n. 13, J. Migne, *Patrologia Latina*, XXXVIII, 923.
[57] *Only Jesus*, p. 22.
[58] Romans 8, 28.

Chapter Six

Angels

Since love often inclines one to share, God created spirits with intellect and free will, but without bodies called *angels,* and *humans* who have a body, soul, intellect, and free will.

The word *angel* is derived from the Greek word for *messenger.* Angels are divided into nine choirs (groups): Angels, Archangels, Thrones, Dominations, Virtues, Principalities, Powers, Cherubim, and Seraphim. They have special talents and fulfill specific roles including adoring God, assisting humans and serving as Guardian Angels. St. Bernard describes angels as:

> ...spirits, mighty, glorious, blessed, distinct personalities, of graduated rank, ...endowed with immortality, ...being of pure mind, benignant affections, religious and devout; of unblemished morality... blessed with unbroken peace.[59]

God tested the angels in order to prove their fidelity. Theologians believe that they were commanded to adore the God-Man, Jesus Christ. Lucifer, the most gifted angel, who was filled with pride, began a rebellion against God. Instead of honoring Christ, he wanted to place *his* throne in Heaven and be worshipped as God as the prophet Isaias relates: "I will ascend into Heaven. I will exalt my throne above the stars of God. I will be like the Most High."[60]

Devils

Sacred Scripture (the Bible) tells us that one third of the angels joined Lucifer,[61] including many from the choirs of Principalities and Powers as related by St. Paul:

> ...our wrestling is not against flesh and blood, but against the Principalities and the Powers, against world rulers of darkness, against the forces of wickedness on high.[62]

Heroic St. Michael rallied the faithful angels and cried, "Who is like unto God?" Lucifer and his rebellious angels were instantly cast into the fires of Hell where they will remain forever. Jesus spoke of this when He said, "I saw Satan [Lucifer] like lightning falling from Heaven."[63]

Fallen angels, also called devils, demons or bad angels have a will that is irreversible. They will never ask pardon for disobeying God and therefore, cannot be redeemed. The ultimate goal of devils, who often resemble flies that pester and annoy, is to lead souls to Hell. The word *Beelzebub* means *Lord of Flies.* Interestingly, the word "evil" is "devil" without the letter "d."

Using their great intelligence and power, devils often disguise themselves as angels of light[64] to deceive and mislead. Devils are creatures that are subject to God. He limits their power so they can only do what God permits.

God provides effective means to combat demons and fight temptation. St. Paul said to "put on the armor of light."[65] These spiritual weapons include devout prayer (especially the Rosary), reception of the Sacraments of Penance and the Holy Eucharist, recitation of Pope Leo XIII's Prayer to St. Michael, holy water, and the invocation of the holy names of Jesus and Mary.

---

[59] *De Consideratione,* Lib. V, ch. 4.
[60] Chapter 14, Verse 13.
[61] See Apocalypse 12, 4. "This is spoken with an illusion to the fall of Lucifer from Heaven, with the rebellious angels, driven from thence by St. Michael." Catholic commentary by Fr. Leo Haydock, *Douay Rheims Bible,* p. 1641.
[62] Ephesians 6, 12.
[63] Luke 10, 18 f.
[64] 2 Corinthians 11, 14.
[65] Romans 13, 12.

Although some blame their sins on the devil, individuals are responsible for their own actions. Satan once complained to St. Anthony the Abbot about the matter.

> I am often not so much to blame as you think, for people are often the cause of their own ruin, by seeking the occasions of sin, hoping that they will not fall, although they know how frail they are. I never could overcome them if they only used the weapons God has put into their hands. So they need not blame me, nor curse me so much, since it is entirely their own fault that they are lost.[66]

The Devils and their Evil Works

Many today practice Satanism and Wicca, while others thoughtlessly join in practices that have diabolical roots. Satanic video games, Ouija Boards, yoga, heavy metal music, horoscopes, and tarot cards are sinful and very dangerous since they often lead one to delve into witchcraft, develop a fascination with Satan or cause one to reject God.

Yoga is not merely a form of exercise and stretching. Its roots are based in Buddhism and Hinduism. Heavy Metal groups actively promote Satanism through their lyrics, band names, pentagrams, satanic symbols, and concerts.

Diabolical possession can occur as a result of these activities, or by a spell, curse or other means. When a person is possessed by the devil, God permits evil spirits to enter and control the individual's body, although one still has a free will.

Obsession is the word used to describe attacks by the devil from without, including hearing sinister voices, major distractions during prayers and physical attacks with no visible culprit.

The Roman Ritual lists various ways to detect the devil's presence in a person including knowledge of hidden things and unknown languages, superhuman strength, and hatred of God, Mary, the saints, and anything sacred.

Exorcism, derived from the word *exit,* means *to go out.* Devils can be driven out of a possessed person or a building infested with demons by Catholic clergy through exorcism prayers like the Prayer to St. Michael of Pope Leo XIII and formal exorcism prayers of the *Roman Ritual.* Priests must have permission from their bishop to perform a formal exorcism.

The Fourth Lateran Council in 1215 taught that the fallen angels were created good by God, but that they made themselves evil.[67] Devils freely chose to disobey God and never repented. Unrepentant humans act in like manner by not being sorry for their sins. Both cases demonstrate bad will and merit punishment.

Guardian Angels

Angels who remained faithful to God were rewarded with the eternal happiness of Heaven. They love and serve God and act as friends and protectors of human beings. "The Angel of the Lord shall encamp round about them that fear Him and shall deliver them."[68]

God desires the eternal salvation of all and loves everyone so much that He gives each person a Guardian Angel to protect, inspire and guard them from temptation. People should often pray

---

[66] Very Rev. Canon Howe, *Stories from the Catechist,* p. 145.
[67] Denzinger 427-428.
[68] Psalm 33.

to their Guardian Angel, a powerful and dear friend who will help them get to Heaven. "For He has given His angels charge over thee in all thy ways."[69]

Jesus referred to Guardian Angels when he warned His followers of the severe judgment awaiting those who scandalize children, "...for I say to you that their angels in Heaven always see the face of My Father Who is in heaven."[70]

Role of Angels

Angels are not just passive bystanders. They are present throughout history and are active in our lives today. These blessed spirits who enjoy perfect happiness, serve and glorify God and assist humans. Angels rejoice when souls return to God as St. Luke relates, "...there shall be joy before the angels of God upon one sinner doing penance."[71]

Archangels

Three archangels are mentioned in Scripture—St. Michael, St. Gabriel and St. Raphael. This honorary title declares that they rank above the other angels as God's special emissaries.

St. Michael leads the angels and cast Lucifer and the devils into Hell. St. Gabriel at the Annunciation asked Mary for her consent to become the Mother of the Redeemer. St. Raphael, the healer, is mentioned in the Book of Tobias.[72]

Angels Mentioned in the Bible

The Old and New Testaments of Scripture relate many examples of how angels protected God's people and delivered them from harm, even against unbelievable odds. The Book of Exodus records God's admonition to the Chosen People regarding angels:

> Behold I will send my angel who shall go before thee, and keep thee in thy journey, and bring thee into the place that I have prepared. Take notice of him and hear his voice, and do not think him one to be contemned.[73]

Angels daily assist people all over the world protecting them from accidents and serious injury, guiding and helping them overcome temptation, and raising their hearts to God. In Heaven, people will understand how helpful their Guardian Angels have been to them. The Bible mentions many accounts of angelic assistance.

Around the year 700 BC, King Sennacherib's Assyrian army encircled Jerusalem as the monarch blasphemously challenged God and those who believed in Him by saying:

> In whom do you trust [Ezechias, King of Juda], that you sit still besieged in Jerusalem? ...Know you not what I and my fathers have done to all the people of the lands?

> ...For if no god of all the nations and kingdoms, could deliver his people out of my hand, and out of the hand of my fathers, consequently neither shall your God be able to deliver you out of my hand?[74]

---

[69] Psalm 90, 11.
[70] Mark 18, 10.
[71] Chapter 15, Verse 10.
[72] Chapter 3, Verse 25.
[73] Chapter 23, Verses 20-21.
[74] 2 Paralipomenon 32, 10, 13, 15.

God intervened by sending a single angel who eliminated the threat by annihilating 185,000 Assyrians. Providentially, God rewarded the faith of the starving Hebrews by replenishing their food supplies with that left by their enemies. Sennacherib returned to the pagan temple in Nineveh where he was slain by his two sons.

An angel told Zachary in the temple that his wife, St. Elizabeth, would become the mother of St. John the Baptist. Another angel spoke to St. Joseph and told him that Mary conceived by the Holy Ghost. One of God's heavenly messengers later warned him to escape to Egypt with the Holy Family because Herod ordered the massacre of newborns. Angels were present at the Birth of Our Lord, during Jesus' Agony in the Garden, His Resurrection, and Ascension.

Chapter Seven

Humans

Humans Have a Higher Destiny

Human beings are God's greatest creation on earth. The *Baltimore Catechism* says, "Man is a creature composed of body and soul, and made to the image and likeness of God."[75] Humans differ from other creatures by being able to think and freely choose their actions. God gave humans dominion over the earth that He created to serve their needs.

Animals, on the other hand, do not possess reason but rely on instinct for their survival and preservation. Have you ever seen a deer look both ways before crossing a street?

People intuitively know they have a higher destiny than life on earth, though many focus on riches, pleasure and material possessions. Humans who glorify God by knowing, loving and serving Him on earth will be rewarded with the eternal happiness of Heaven.

Following God's Plan

God demands each person to be responsible for his or her actions. Although He bestows innumerable talents and benefits, the essentials of life and grace, it is up to each individual to follow His laws and love God and neighbor, or reject them, and suffer the consequences.

Humans desire happiness, but it can be found in God alone. Unfortunately, the devil tempts people to harden their consciences and think that they are not responsible for their actions in order to justify their selfish, sinful lifestyle.

Good Catholics live by faith and keep their eyes focused on Heaven. Their beliefs affect the way they live, their morals and everyday activities. St. Thomas Aquinas compares faith to a light that helps individuals see what they believe.

Catholics try not to be controlled by circumstances, but use them as a means of practicing virtue and being faithful to God, Who gives grace and interior peace of soul in return. Even though it is not always popular to do what is right, every individual will ultimately have to answer to God. It is more important to make it to Heaven than be well liked on earth.

Adam and Eve

God created the first man, Adam, and said: "It is not good for man to be alone: let Us make a help like unto himself."[76] He then created Eve and instituted marriage saying: "Wherefore a man shall leave father and mother, and shall cleave to his wife and they shall be two in one flesh."[77] They and their offspring were created with a mortal[78] body and immortal[79] soul.

Psalm 8 verses 6-10 relates that humans were given dominion over the earth.

> Thou hast made him a little less than the angels, thou hast crowned him with glory and honor: and hast set him over the works of thy hands. Thou hast subjected all things under his feet, all sheep and oxen: moreover the beasts also of the fields. The birds of the air, and the fishes of the sea, that pass through the paths of the sea.

---

[75] p. 32.
[76] Genesis 2, 18.
[77] Genesis 2, 24.
[78] A body that will eventually die.
[79] The human soul will never die.

God created humans to know, love, and serve Him, to show forth His goodness and to share His everlasting happiness in Heaven with them.[80]

Adam and Eve were Given Special Gifts from God

Natural	human body / immortal soul	intellect and free will
Preternatural	infused knowledge and faculties *beyond* normal human nature	
Supernatural	sanctifying grace	a sharing in the life of God

The Fall

God placed Adam and Eve in the Garden of Paradise where they were perfectly happy. Adam, representing the entire human race, was given a simple test. If he followed God's command, he and his offspring would be rewarded. If he disobeyed, he and they would be punished.

God commanded our first parents not to eat fruit from a certain tree in Paradise. Satan, disguised as a talking snake, persuaded Eve to disobey God's order by telling her "that in what day soever you shall eat thereof, your eyes shall be opened: and you shall be like Gods..."[81] She then coaxed Adam to disobey by consuming the fruit.

This serious act of disobedience by Adam against God is called *original sin* because it comes to us through our origin, Adam. St. Paul wrote: "By one man sin entered the world, and by sin, death, and so death passed upon all men, in whom we have all sinned."[82]

God was angered and asked Adam why he had disregarded His explicit command. Adam blamed Eve and she blamed the snake. The guilt and punishment of Adam's sin descends from him to his posterity.[83] They should have admitted their guilt and asked pardon of God.

God Punished Adam, Eve and their Offspring

- They lost sanctifying[84] grace, the greatest gift they received, a sharing in the life of God.

- Adam and Eve were cast out of Paradise.

- The Gates of Heaven were closed.

- Childbirth would become painful.

- Adam and Eve lost all the preternatural gifts they received.

- Humans would have to work to feed and support themselves.

- Human beings would be subject to disease, illness and death.

- Adam and Eve and all human beings acquired a tendency to evil called *concupiscence*.

- Adam and Eve lost the gift of integrity—complete subjection of the passions to reason.

---

[80] See *Baltimore Catechism,* Lesson Five.
[81] Genesis 3, 5.
[82] Romans 5, 22.
[83] See *Catechism of the Council of Trent,* original sin.
[84] Taken from two Latin words that mean: *to make holy.*

Chapter Eight
The Redeemer
The Incarnation

Due to the fall of Adam, it was necessary that a Redeemer atone for original sin and for the sins of his descendants. He needed to have the *nature of God* to satisfy divine justice and the *nature of man* (body and soul) to make adequate atonement on their behalf. The only way the Messias could suffer, thereby manifesting His love for mankind, was to assume human nature.

The *Incarnation* refers to Jesus assuming a human nature when the Second Person of the Blessed Trinity, sent by the Father, was conceived in the womb of Mary by the overshadowing of the Holy Ghost at the Annunciation.

Our Lord Jesus Christ

The *Baltimore Catechism* teaches: "...the Son of God retaining His divine nature, took to Himself a human nature, that is, a body and soul like ours."[85] The union of the divine nature and the human nature in one Person, Jesus Christ, is called the *hypostatic union*.[86] Our Lord's two natures are described in chapter one of St. John's Gospel, read daily at the Latin Mass.[87]

Jesus redeemed mankind, opened the Gates of Heaven and offered all[88] the graces necessary for salvation by His Life, Passion[89] and Death on the Cross. St. John wrote that Christ loved us and washed us from our sins in His Blood.[90] Yet, in spite of this, each person must cooperate with God's grace in order to merit eternal happiness.

How did the Savior, Jesus Christ, enter the world? Since He is the Son of God, He could have come as a grown man and atoned for the sins of mankind by a simple prayer. Yet, Our Lord, the Second Person of the Blessed Trinity, came to earth humbly. He taught, showed the way to Heaven, and instituted the Catholic Church. What a wondrous proof of God's love!

The name *Jesus* is derived from the Hebrew word for *Savior*. *Christ* is the Greek word for *Anointed One*. Although Our Lord Jesus Christ lived on earth for 33 years, He spent only three years teaching. The first 30 years are called His *Hidden Life*.

Jesus was the greatest miracle worker that ever lived. *A miracle is a supernatural occurrence affected by Divine power.* Christ is not just a holy man from Nazareth. He is the Son of God equal to the Father and the Holy Ghost, having the same nature.

St. John the Baptist told his disciples they would know that Jesus was the Messias by witnessing His miracles. "The blind see, the lame walk, the lepers are cleansed, the deaf hear, the dead rise again, the poor have the Gospel preached to them."[91]

Our Lord's Public Life was filled with miracles. His first public miracle occurred at the Marriage of Cana when He changed water into wine, something that is chemically impossible. Christ healed the sick and paralytics, walked on water, miraculously fed thousands, and calmed a storm at sea.

---

[85] p. 49.
[86] Pope Pius XI in the encyclical *Lux Veritatis* explained hypostatic as "the marvelous and substantial union of the two natures."
[87] Commonly called the Last Gospel because it is the second Gospel read at Mass.
[88] "God... Who wishes all men to be saved and come to the knowledge of the truth." 1 Timothy 2, 4. All are redeemed and given sufficient grace to be saved, but individuals must cooperate with God's grace and keep the commandments to save their soul.
[89] Taken from a Latin word meaning *sufferings*.
[90] Apocalypse 1, 5.
[91] Matthew 11, 5.

Christ's Public Life

Some wanted the Messias to be a political leader who would rid Palestine of Roman overlords. Jesus' mission was to save souls and redeem mankind, teaching by word and example.

No one ever had such a dramatic effect on history as Jesus Christ. Until recently, the annals of mankind were measured by the notations BC (Before Christ) and AD (*in anno Domini*, in the year of the Lord).

Jesus Christ founded His Church on Twelve Apostles and inspired Hebrews and Gentiles, just and sinners to become members. His teachings are found in the Gospels written by the Evangelists—*Matthew, Mark, Luke, and John.* The Holy Sacrifice of the Mass was instituted by Our Lord to mystically renew in an unbloody manner His Passion and Death on the Cross. Christ instituted Seven Sacraments, outward signs that signify the inner graces they bestow. Therefore, since Christ's teachings, the Mass and sacraments are of divine origin, no one on earth has power to essentially change them.

The Redemption

Jesus atoned for the pride of Adam, Eve and their offspring by His life of poverty and humility. During His Agony at the Garden of Gethsemane, Jesus sweat blood at the sight of all the sins of the world that would be committed. Our Lord was scourged, had a crown of thorns pressed upon His head and carried a wooden cross that weighed about 100 pounds nearly a quarter of a mile to Mt. Calvary in Jerusalem. There He willingly died by suffocation and loss of blood in order to atone for the sins of the world and open the Gates of Heaven.

On the first Good Friday, many mocked Jesus, while others challenged Him to come down from the Cross. Our Lord chose to manifest His divinity in other ways. During the three hours He hung on the Cross, the entire earth was covered in darkness, a great earthquake occurred and many holy persons from the past emerged from their tombs. Also, the temple veil ripped in half, signifying the end of the Old Testament and the beginning of the New.

Christ made reparation for every sin that was ever committed and endured terrible pain and interior desolation in order to satisfy God's justice and atone for the ingratitude of mankind.

Our Lord entered the world as a baby, was born in a stable, lived in poverty, spent His life doing good to others, and endured terrible suffering culminating in His death on the Cross in order to win our love. No one could ever say God didn't love them or understand their pain.

The Resurrection of Christ

Our Lord did something that no one ever did before and no one has done since. He foretold when He would die, how He would die, and, most miraculous of all, that He would rise again. The Scribes and Pharisees remembered that Jesus said he would rise from the dead. Therefore, after Jesus' death on the Cross, they asked Roman governor Pontius Pilate to order soldiers to guard the tomb[92] in order to prevent anyone from approaching or attempting to steal Christ's body. A huge boulder was then placed over its entrance.

Despite these preventive measures, Our Lord triumphantly emerged from the tomb with a glorified body and remained on earth for 40 days teaching and establishing His Church. He left His burial shroud as a lasting remembrance of His sufferings.

---

[92] See Matthew 28, 65-66

If Our Lord were a mere mortal, His work would have ended with His Death. Jesus appeared to the Apostles after His Resurrection and showed them the radiant marks of His wounds on His hands, feet and side. Those wounds opened the Gates of Heaven and were the price of our redemption. Jesus' Resurrection and Passion manifest God's infinite love.

The Church of the Holy Sepulchre in Jerusalem encompasses both the spot of the crucifixion (Calvary)[93] and the tomb of the Resurrection where pilgrims are edified by the reality of what occurred there 2,000 years earlier. Inside His tomb is a long, narrow stone bench where tradition says the Body of Jesus was laid.

The Holy Shroud

St. John describes two cloths in his Gospel—one wrapping Jesus' Body and another covering His Face. The *Holy Shroud*, an ancient artifact, is a 14-foot long linen cloth that enveloped Christ's crucified Body. The *Sudarium* (facecloth) is preserved in Oviedo, Spain. Many icons of Our Lord were derived from them during the early centuries of the Church.

The Holy Shroud is woven in a herringbone pattern, similar to cloth found at Masada that dates back to 40 BC-73 AD. In 1532, the Holy Shroud was kept at Sainte-Chapelle in Chambéry, France. Although a fire singed the ends of the Shroud, the main image was miraculously untouched. The sacred cloth was later transferred to Turin, Italy in 1578 to the Cathedral of St. John the Baptist where it is preserved in a transparent case.

Internal and external evidence attest to the authenticity of the Holy Shroud. Scientists from Israel and Switzerland found that the cloth contains pollen grains and images from plants native to Jerusalem which have bloomed in Israel between March and May for thousands of years. Similar pollen grains have also been found on the Sudarium of Oviedo.

The cloth shows clear evidence of Our Lord's Passion including severe wounds from a Roman flagrum,[94] puncture wounds about His head indicating where a crown of thorns was placed, a bruised kneecap, and broken nasal cartilage, the result of beatings and numerous falls.

Remarkably, the image, that is three-dimensional, mostly resides in a layer at the surface of the linen. There is no trace of paint pigmentation and its origin still baffles scientists.

Dark stains on the Holy Shroud have been identified as human blood and there are clear marks made from nails through the wrists and feet. The side wound into the heart is the exact size of the tip of a Roman lance. The attention to detail in all areas is beyond the skill of the most talented forger.

Traces of writing in Aramaic, Greek and Latin are present on the cloth. Coins, minted during the time of Tiberius (42 BC–37 AD) and containing the image of Pontius Pilate, were placed over Jesus' eyes at His burial. The Holy Shroud is the most examined artifact on the planet. The more skeptical scientists attempt to discredit it, the more its veracity shines forth.

In 1898, Secunda Pia took the first photographs of the Shroud. The image of the crucified Christ appeared clearly visible on the negative glass plate he used in his darkroom.

---

[93] Place of the skull. Tradition relates that the bottom of Jesus' Cross rested on Adam's skull that was buried below.
[94] A whip with short leather thongs tipped with pieces of bronze or lead.

Eighty years later, scientists from the Shroud of Turin Research Project (STURP) were given full access for five days to perform countless tests that further authenticated the burial cloth. The Shroud continues to be studied and examined.

In 2010, Ray Downing, a computer artist and inventor of highly advanced computer technology, produced a remarkable three-dimensional image of the face of Christ from the Shroud. Scientists are baffled by the Shroud since it is not a painting, drawing, scorch mark, or photograph. The increasingly sophisticated technology used for testing has not discredited its authenticity, but rather affirmed it.

The Ascension

When Our Lord's work was completed, He rose into the sky from the summit of Mt. Olivet by His own power and disappeared from sight. Our Lord is the way, the truth and the life; no one comes to the Father, except through Him.[95]

Jesus Christ founded the Catholic Church that will last until the end of time. Miraculously, His Church, the Catholic[96] Church, remains essentially the same as when He established it nearly 2,000 years ago.

Attacks Against the Divinity of Christ

There have been numerous attacks against the Divinity of Christ that have been condemned by the Church. Christianity becomes meaningless if Jesus is not the Son of God equal to the Father and the Holy Ghost.

Arius   blasphemously said Jesus was a holy man, not the Son of God nor equal to the Father.
            Condemned by the First Council of Nicaea in 325 AD

Nestorius heretically claimed Mary was not the Mother of God.
            Condemned by the Council of Ephesus in 431 AD

Eutyches erroneously taught that Jesus had only one nature, not two, human and divine.
            Condemned by the Council of Chalcedon in 451 AD

Sergius   falsely taught that Jesus had only one will, not two, a human will and a divine will.
            Condemned by the Third Council of Constantinople in 681 AD

Manmade Religions Fade with Time

There have been myriads of manmade religions. During the French Revolution, two were formed called the Cult of Reason and the Cult of the Supreme Being, a non-Christian religion invented by Robespierre.

When the revolutionary Reveillere (1753-1824) thought of starting a humanist, deist religion, he shared the idea with a government official named Barras requesting his advice on the best way to propagate it. Barras merely repeated a phrase from Voltaire: "Well, my advice is to get killed on Friday, and rise from the dead on Sunday."[97] No trace of this religion remains today.

---

[95] John 14, 6.
[96] *Catholic* is derived from the Greek word for *universal*. St. Ignatius of Antioch first used *catholic* to describe followers of Christ.
[97] See Rev. F. Drinkwater, *Catechism Stories, Part I, The Creed*, p. 55.

Chapter Nine
The Blessed Virgin Mary
Prophesies Fulfilled

God promised to send a Messias who would atone for original sin and the sins of mankind and open the Gates of Heaven. "I will put enmities between thee [Satan] and the woman [Mary] and thy seed and her seed. She shall crush thy head and thou shalt lie in wait for her heel."[98]

Numerous prophecies foretold the Redeemer and His mission. The entire world waited in anticipation for 4,000 years for the coming of the Messias, a period annually recalled by the liturgical season of Advent, the four weeks before Christmas.

Christ fulfilled prophecies that were foretold centuries earlier. He was born of a virgin of the House of David,[99] in Bethlehem[100] and three monarchs, led to the stable cave by a star, came to worship Him.[101] Only a God-man could choose the place and other details of His birth.

The Immaculate Conception

Our Lady was sinless and *immaculately conceived without original sin.* She was conceived by her parents in a natural manner, but preserved from original sin.

Pope Pius IX extolled Mary's glories in his encyclical on the Immaculate Conception:

> The Lord endowed Mary with such an abundance of graces that she surpassed by far all the angels and saints; thus the Blessed Virgin has such fullness of innocence and of sanctity that it can be found and thought of in a greater degree only in God.[102]

The Annunciation

Mary made a vow of virginity when very young that God allowed her to miraculously preserve. When the angel St. Gabriel asked Mary if she would consent to be the Mother of the Redeemer, the long-awaited Messias, he reassured her she would remain a virgin. He greeted her with the words, "Hail, full of grace, the Lord is with thee. Blessed art thou among women."[103]

The *Catechism of the Council of Trent* describes this wondrous event:

> ...as soon as the Blessed Virgin assented to the announcement of the angel in these words, *Behold the handmaid of the Lord; be it done unto me according to thy word,* the most sacred body of Christ was immediately formed, and to it was united a rational soul enjoying the use of reason and thus in the same instant of time He was perfect God and perfect man. That this was the astonishing and admirable work of the Holy Ghost cannot be doubted.[104]

The Virgin / Mother of God

The Blessed Virgin was the means chosen by God to bring Christ into this world. Isaias explained Mary's role of virgin-mother: "Behold, a Virgin shall conceive and bear a Son, and His name shall be called Emmanuel;"[105] "which is interpreted God with us."[106]

---

[98] Genesis 3, 15.
[99] Isaias 11, 1.
[100] Micheas 5, 2.
[101] Isaias 60, 6.
[102] *Ineffabilis Deus,* December 8, 1854. The Immaculate Conception and Divine Maternity of Mary are dogmas of the Church.
[103] Luke 1, 28.
[104] p. 43.
[105] Isaias 7, 14.
[106] Matthew 1, 23.

The Blessed Virgin is the only woman in history who was a virgin-mother. God arranged this so she could be an exemplary model for virgins and mothers. Mary was completely sinless, remained a virgin and conceived Christ by the overshadowing of the Holy Ghost. Christ dwelt in her womb for nine months.

Jesus' birth was painless and He miraculously preserved her virginity. Mary remained always a virgin, before, during and after the birth of Christ. Some saints compare Jesus' birth to light passing through glass.

Mary is rightfully called Mother of God because the Second Person of the Blessed Trinity, Jesus Christ, is her Son. Pope Pius XI wrote that the life of Our Lord manifested

> ...clear evidence of two natures in Christ, from which proceed works that are divine and human, and shows also very clearly that Christ is one, God and man alike through the unity of the divine Person by which He is called *Theantropos* [God-Man].[107]

St. Cyril of Alexandria describes the Divine Maternity.

> Not that the nature or divinity of the Word [Christ] took its origin or beginning from the holy Virgin, but in this sense that He derived from her His Sacred Body, born... and perfected by an intelligent soul to which the Word of God was hypostatically united.[108]

Pope Leo XIII encourages the Faithful to revere the Virgin, Mother of God, through the devout recitation of the Rosary.[109] Fr. Tanquerey says:

> From the dignity of the Divine maternity proceed all the privileges granted to the Blessed Virgin, her most perfect sanctity, and her supernatural relations with creatures [as intercessor].[110]

The Role of Mary

Since Mary united her sufferings with those of Jesus on the Cross, she is called co-Redemptrix. Pope St. Pius X said that God rewarded the Blessed Virgin by making her the dispensatrix of all the graces that Christ merited by His sufferings.

St. Bernardine of Siena writes:

> Every grace granted to man has three successive steps: By God it is communicated to Christ, from Christ it passes to the Virgin, and from the Virgin it descends to us.[111]

Mary's Assistance Now and at the Hour of Death

Our Lady told St. Bridget of Sweden that she comes to assist her children as soon as they call on her. Mary is addressed in the *Hail Holy Queen* as *our life, our sweetness and our hope.*

St. Alphonsus Liguori and St. Louis de Montfort teach that the Blessed Virgin Mary is frequently present at the deathbed of those who have been devoted to her. The Heavenly Mother calms her child, prepares the soul to enter eternity and wards off demons that make their last attempt to snatch it away from God.

---

[107] Encyclical *Lux Veritatis,* December 25, 1931.
[108] Mansi, *Conciliorum Amplissima Collectio IV,* circa 1007, 891.
[109] *Adjutricem Populi,* September 5, 1895
[110] *Manual of Dogmatic Theology: Two,* p. 99
[111] *Serm.* 6, n. I, *in Fest.* BMV, de Ann., a. I, c. 2, Pope Leo XIII, *Juncunda Semper,* September 8, 1894.

Chapter Ten

Grace

"Grace is a supernatural gift of God bestowed on us through the merits of Jesus Christ for our salvation."[112] St. Thomas Aquinas wrote that grace is a gratuitous gift, a sign of God's favor, and makes the recipient one of God's favorites.[113]

The Need for Grace

Jesus taught the vital need for grace. Since Our Lord merited all graces, He emphatically said, "...without Me you can do nothing."[114] St. Paul taught "By grace you have been saved through faith; and that not from yourselves, for it is the gift of God."[115]

Due to original sin, people have a strong tendency to evil called concupiscence that must be controlled. Guided by human nature alone, one naturally descends into a life of sin. The world entices people to abandon God and "enjoy life" by making vice enticing and virtue appear "out of style."

The Spiritual Combat

Devils plot to lead individuals into serious sin. God's grace is necessary for people to practice supernatural virtue and observe the Ten Commandments. Grace fortifies individuals during this battle, the saints call the *spiritual combat.*

The *Catechism of the Council of Trent* describes the need for grace:

> But such is the degeneracy of our nature [due to concupiscence] that, even when we have done violence to our passions and subjected them to the will of God, we cannot avoid sin without His assistance, by which we are protected from evil and directed in the pursuit of good.[116]

God does not leave one defenseless, but offers spiritual weapons. These means of grace include prayer, the Mass, sacraments, and sacramentals. These form a type of protective wall to help shield one from the allurement of temptation and occasions of sin.

Actual Grace

Actual grace is a supernatural help from God that enlightens the mind and strengthens the will to help one do good and avoid evil.[117] Although all do not use His gifts of grace, God *gives everyone* sufficient grace to be saved and reach Heaven. St. Paul says that God, "...wills all men to be saved, and to come to the knowledge of the truth."[118]

Saints compare actual grace to a mist that falls upon the earth healing the soul from the effects of sin and helping one persevere in the performance of good works.

Those who utilize God's grace become saints. As water can either invigorate (living things), or be discarded so the gift of grace can be accepted or rejected. Grace is precious, not something to be wasted or spurned. If grace is consistently rejected, God often withdraws His help unless the individual repents before death.

---

[112] Rev. Thomas Kinkead, *Baltimore Catechism, No. 4,* p. 102
[113] *Summa Theologica,* I-II ae, q. 110, Respond.
[114] John 15, 5.
[115] Ephesians 2, 8.
[116] p. 536.
[117] See Fr. Connell, *Baltimore Catechism No. 3,* p. 63.
[118] 1 Timothy 2, 4.

St. Cyprian said God offers His assistance and protection to those who pray so they can practice virtue and resist sin. St. Augustine wrote, as the eye needs light for proper vision, so the just need God's grace in order to persevere in doing good.

Sanctifying Grace

Sanctifying grace is a sharing in the life of God. St. Thomas Aquinas calls it, "a certain beauty of the soul which wins the divine favor."[119] Catholics first receive sanctifying grace at Baptism. Our Lord described it as the pearl of great price, the wedding garment necessary to enter Heaven and a treasure more precious than all the riches of the world.

Sanctifying grace is lost when one commits a mortal sin. It is regained by the Sacrament of Penance if one is truly sorry and firmly resolves never to sin again. Thomas a' Kempis wrote:

> For the gifts of nature are common to the good and the bad; but grace or divine love, is the proper gift of the elect and they that are adorned with it are esteemed worthy of eternal life.[120]

Kempis calls grace, "...the light of the heart, the comforter of the afflicted, the banisher of sorrow, the expeller of fears, the nurse of devotion."[121]

Sanctifying grace is a treasure of infinite value—one's ticket to Heaven. This grace is increased in the soul by prayer, attendance at Mass and reception of the sacraments.

Without sanctifying grace, one cannot enter Heaven. Therefore, it must be preserved at all costs since the world, fallen human nature and the devil constantly try to rob the faithful of this pearl of great price.

Fall from Grace

Since most falls from grace are gradual, many don't even realize how far they have drifted. St. Paul warns the proud, complacent and those who presume on God's mercy: "...let him who thinks he stands take heed lest he fall."[122]

Some return to God by persevering effort and regain peace of soul and inner joy. Others, like exhausted scuba divers who have to make a long surface swim in order to reach their dive boat, give up hope and are swallowed by the waves. All these divers had to do was get close to the boat and a ring buoy could have been tossed to them. Often help is only a prayer away.

Faithful to the End

Prayer draws down God's graces and is essential for one to persevere in doing good and avoiding evil.[123] The Council of Trent says that *final perseverance* is a gift that God bestows on those who pray.[124] Only God can give someone supernatural courage to calmly approach death when life ends and eternity begins. Some even have a heavenly look in their eyes at death that reflects the indescribable joys experienced in the next life.

A mother once died peacefully after receiving the Last Sacraments. Several days later her son heard the words said in her gentle voice, "I've never known such joy." What an inspiring manifestation of God's goodness and the immense happiness of Heaven!

---

[119] *Summa Theologica* 1-2, 110, 2.
[120] *The Imitation of Christ,* Part 3, Chapter 55.
[121] Part 3, Chapter 55.
[122] 1 Corinthians 10, 12.
[123] See Canons 9-10 of the Second Council of Orange.
[124] See Denzinger 832.

Chapter Eleven

Faith

The Councils of Vienne and Trent [125] taught that sanctifying grace and the theological virtues of faith, hope and charity are infused into the soul at Baptism. *Faith allows one to firmly believe the truths God has revealed.*[126] St. Francis de Sales in his *Works (Oeuvres)* wrote: "Faith can be said to be nothing else but an adhesion of the understanding and will to divine truths." St. Ambrose called faith the foundation of all virtues.

Natural Faith

Electricity, wind and sound are invisible, but real. People believe by natural faith the words their boss, reporters, law enforcement officers, researchers, and others say. On the testimony of others, they accept the existence of countries, planets and oceans they have never seen.

Many today believe only what they see and persist in unreasonable skepticism. They fail to realize absolute certainty is seldom and frequently impossible to attain and human reason is not always a reliable guide. Faulty or insufficient information, prejudice and rash judgment often warp a person's judgment. Others "read" into facts to suit their purpose.

Supernatural Faith

Pope Leo XIII said by means of faith "man is raised above nature and is endowed with dispositions requisite for life eternal."[127] Supernatural faith illuminates one's path in a changing world and shows the real meaning of life. It directs a person on the path to God and true, lasting happiness. Disappointments and difficulties lose much of their bitterness once one sees their value toward meriting an eternal reward hereafter.

Our Lord said: "Blessed are they who have not seen, and yet have believed"[128] and "Unless you turn and become like little children, you will not enter the Kingdom of Heaven."[129] He wants His followers to believe His teachings with childlike simplicity and humble faith.

By means of faith, belief is not based solely on the Word of God, not external evidence, thereby giving absolute certitude in religious matters for God can neither deceive, nor be deceived.

God gave humans intellect and free will so they could act without compulsion, not like programmed robots. Faith is a free act of the will that manifests deep love for God and trust in His word. It reassures the believer and gives meaning to life.

The Need for Faith

St. Paul stressed the importance of faith when he wrote, "...my just one lives by faith."[130] Martin Luther erroneously based his religion on faith alone. St. James refuted this ideology when he wrote in his epistle that faith must be accompanied by a good life.

> What will it profit, my brethren, if a man says he has faith, but does not have works? Can the faith save him? So faith too, unless it has works, is dead in itself.[131]

---

[125] Denzinger 483 and 800.
[126] See: Rev. Thomas Kinkead, *Baltimore Catechism, No. 4,* Question 107, p. 104.
[127] *Adjutricem Populi*, September 5, 1895.
[128] John 20, 29.
[129] Matthew 18, 3.
[130] Epistle to the Hebrews 10, 38.
[131] Chapter 2, Verses 14-17.

St. Cyril of Jerusalem said:

> The power of faith is enormous. It is so great that it not only saves the believer: thanks to one person's faith others are saved also [led to sanctity by their example].

Pleasure

Faith helps one differentiate between pleasure and happiness. Those who seek pleasure look in the wrong places and never find happiness. Life without God is empty.

Pleasure is enjoyment experienced through the five senses. It can be good (reading an inspirational story), indifferent (enjoying a nice meal) or sinful (viewing pornography). Pleasure only lasts for a time and can become distasteful when prolonged.

Happiness

Although everyone desires peace and happiness, these are something only God can give.[132] These impart an inner tranquility with God, with oneself and one's neighbor. St. Augustine teaches, the greatest possible happiness comes from the possession of the truth.[133]

Perfect happiness can only be found in Heaven since God is the ultimate source of happiness. "It consists in the vision of God and enjoyment of His beauty Who is the source and principle of all goodness and perfection."[134]

Peace of Soul

The angels at Christmas spoke of this peace when they said "...on earth peace among men of good will."[135] Jesus said, "Peace I leave with you, My peace I give you; not as the world gives do I give to you."[136] This peace does not mean life without difficulties; it means interior peace of soul that helps one handle the problems of life.

Peace of soul can be compared to someone safely standing inside a lighthouse as waves pummel the shoreline. Although the tempest rages outside, the person remains tranquil inside. Human weakness remains to keep one humble, yet, in spite of this, a person knows that God will always intervene and assist when asked.

Having faith can be compared to the difference between being in a storm and watching it on the Weather Channel. Faith gives a person a true perspective of life to proceed confidently forward. Lack of faith leaves people foundering and left to their own devices.

Union with God

A soul faithful to God is like a recently watered plant that basks in the sun. It has everything it needs. Water symbolizes the life of grace within. It is nourished by prayer that draws down God's blessings. When storms occur, roots grow deeper since trials patiently borne deepen one's faith and confidence in God.

---

[132] "If we desire to have *true happiness* on earth, there is no better way than to cultivate piety... Peace of soul, the joy of a good conscience, the happiness of union with God, of growing in His love, of effecting a closer intimacy with Christ, such are a few of the rewards which, along with the comforting hope of life eternal, God dispenses even now to His faithful servants in the midst of their trials." Very Rev. Adolfe Tanquerey, SS, DD, *The Spiritual Life*, p. 182.

[133] *De Lib. Arbitr.* L. II, c. 13, n. 35.

[134] *Catechism of the Council of Trent*, p. 136.

[135] Luke 2, 14.

[136] John 14, 27.

Chapter Twelve

Hope

Hope is the divine virtue by which one firmly trusts that God will give eternal life and the means to obtain it.[137] It reassures a person that God cares and sees every action, and reminds an individual there is an eternal reward for living a virtuous life.

This trust in God gives great merit to the simplest actions and inspires one to heroism and to perseverance in doing good. It also helps a person overcome obstacles and faithfully accomplish what God asks.

Hope Inspires a Person to Progress Spiritually

Trust, fidelity and love are the foundations of a good marriage since they inspire couples to love their spouse unreservedly. Similarly, a soul needs to have unbounded confidence in God to remain faithful to Him and keep the commandments. Thomas a' Kempis, the fifteenth century author of *The Imitation of Christ*, encourages souls to persevere in virtue since "It is no small matter to lose or gain the kingdom of Heaven."[138]

One way to arrive at this goal is to seriously reflect on God's almighty power and infinite mercy and promises—being created by God, redeemed by Jesus' dying on the Cross and realizing perfect happiness in Heaven awaits those who persevere.

By viewing the magnificent world God created—the sun, moon, stars, sky, trees, lakes, rivers, mountains, waterfalls, vegetation, animals, birds, rain, snow, and the cycles of day and night, one can gain greater trust in Him. God Who created all will assist those who invoke Him. "Our help is in the name of the Lord Who created heaven and earth."[139]

Lessons from Scripture

The Book of Judith[140] says "Praise ye the Lord our God, Who hath not forsaken them that hope in Him." Psalm 117 reminds individuals that God is always faithful.

> It is good to confide in the Lord, rather than to have confidence in man. It is good to trust in the Lord rather than to trust in princes.

Israelites in the Old Testament disregarded this advice and turned to the Egyptians for help. Their new friends soon betrayed them.

The Book of Wisdom describes the blessings derived from hoping in God. "They that trust in Him shall understand the truth; and they that are faithful in love shall rest in Him: for grace and peace is to His elect."[141]

Hope is manifested when things appear hopeless. Motives for the virtue of hope include God's power that assures one He can fulfill His promises, His faithfulness assures one that He will fulfill them; and His mercy assures one of His help, in spite of human weakness.

---

[137] See: Rev. Thomas Kinkead, *Baltimore Catechism, No. 4,* question 108, p. 104.
[138] Book III, Chapter 47.
[139] Psalm 123.
[140] Chapter 13, Verse 17.
[141] Chapter 3, Verse 9.

The Book of Daniel gives numerous references to miraculous assistance from God. These include Daniel being delivered from the lion's den; Shadrach, Meshach and Abednego remaining unharmed while inside a fiery furnace, and Suzanna being exonerated when all seemed lost. God takes care of His own. Against all odds, David was victorious over the giant Goliath and centuries later St. Thecla was miraculously protected from hungry lions.

Confidence Despite All

In his book *Secrets of the Interior Life*, Archbishop Luis Martinez describes the childlike attitude of hopeful confidence so pleasing to God in his chapter *Confidence Despite All* where he says we confide in God because of His goodness, mercy and love. St. John Climacus says, "Hope is the power behind love (charity)... When hope fails, so does love."[142]

St. Francis de Sales differentiates between *trust in God* and *presumption* when he said:

> We *hope* for things which it depends on others to bestow, and which we cannot procure ourselves; we *aspire* to those which we can obtain by adopting certain measures. It is chiefly through the grace and mercy of God that we can hope for the enjoyment of His Divine Majesty, yet He requires that we should correspond with His grace by the feeble cooperation of our consent.[143]

Presumption and Despair

Devils deceive millions through presumption and despair, which are the antithesis of hope. *Presumption*, as promoted by Martin Luther, claims a person can lead a sinful life and merely needs to believe in Our Lord to be saved. *Despair*, as taught by Calvin, says a person is predetermined to be saved or damned and there is nothing an individual can do about it. The former makes a mockery of God's laws, the latter leads to hopelessness.

Prayers Answered

During World War II, an American bomber was shot down over the Mediterranean. The sun mercilessly beat down on the wounded survivors who were confined to a small raft. Soon, their food and water supply were exhausted.

With little hope, one of the airmen decided to pray the *Hail Holy Queen* since it was the feast of Mary's Assumption. As they recited the words "turn thine eyes of mercy towards us," they seemed to faintly see something in the distance. It was the periscope of an American submarine that came to rescue them!

Another example of God's providential care took place in the life of missionary Bishop Baraga (1797-1868). Once when he was in the Upper Peninsula of Michigan with a scout on his way to a distant mission, the ice on which they were walking broke away from land and rapidly traveled away from shore.

Adrift on Lake Superior, the largest freshwater lake in the world,[144] the ice float then began to melt and crack. The Snowshoe Bishop remained tranquil in the midst of the peril and prayed to God for assistance. Miraculously the ice took them safely to the Wisconsin shore just a few miles from their planned destination.

---

[142] *The Ladder of Divine Ascent.*
[143] Very Rev. Charles Callan, *Illustrations for Sermons and Instructions,* p. 277.
[144] In area.

Chapter Thirteen

Charity

Love of God and Neighbor

Our Lord defined charity as loving God with one's whole heart, mind, soul, and strength and loving your neighbor as yourself.[145] Love of God is shown in the faithful observance of the commandments. Jesus said: "By this shall all... know that you are My disciples, if you have love for one another"[146] "...as I have loved you, you also love one another."[147]

It takes humility to serve others, to give to those in need and to guide others to a life of virtue. St. John wrote: "...Let us love one another, for love is from God. ...For how can he who does not love his brother, whom he sees, love God, who he does not see?"[148]

Brothers and Sisters

Since all humans share an Eve gene in their DNA,[149] they should treat one another like brother and sister. All individuals trace their genealogy to Adam and Eve, and after the flood, to Noah, his wife and their three sons and wives. There is a natural bond between all humans and a spiritual relationship between members of the Mystical Body of Christ, the Catholic Church.

Social Beings

God created humans as social beings who need to depend on one another for the necessities of life. No one is an island. Christ said to treat everyone with charity and respect.

...love your enemies, do good to those who hate you, and pray for those who persecute and calumniate you, so that you may be children of your Father in Heaven...[150]

The Eight Beatitudes

Jesus gave the Eight Beatitudes at the Sermon on the Mount.[151]

1) Blessed are the poor in spirit, for theirs is the kingdom of Heaven.

2) Blessed are the meek, for they shall possess the earth.

3) Blessed are they who mourn, for they shall be comforted.

4) Blessed are they who hunger and thirst for justice, for they shall be satisfied.

5) Blessed are the merciful, for they shall obtain mercy.

6) Blessed are the clean of heart for they shall see God.

7) Blessed are the peacemakers, for they shall be called children of God.

8) Blessed are they who suffer persecution for justice' sake, for theirs is the kingdom of Heaven.

---

[145] Matthew 22, 37.
[146] John 13, 35.
[147] John 13, 34.
[148] 1 John 4, 7, 20.
[149] "Even more impressive, the geneticists concluded that every person on Earth now can trace his or her lineage back to a common female ancestor..." Taken from—science.howstuffworks.com/life/evolution/female-ancestor.htm "Are we all descended from a common female ancestor?" by Josh Clark. See Ed Wentzel and Vrede van Huyssteen, *Mitochondrial Eve: Encyclopedia of Science and Religion, Vol. 2,* New York: Macmillan Reference USA, 2003, p. 578.
[150] Matthew 5, 44.
[151] Matthew 5, 3-10.

The Catholic Church categorizes charitable works into works of mercy.

Corporal Works of Mercy

1) To feed the hungry

2) To give drink to the thirsty

3) To clothe the naked

4) To visit the imprisoned

5) To shelter the homeless

6) To visit the sick

7) To bury the dead

Spiritual Works of Mercy

1) To admonish the sinner

2) To instruct the ignorant

3) To counsel the doubtful

4) To comfort the sorrowful

5) To bear wrongs patiently

6) To forgive all injuries

7) To pray for the living and the dead

Acts of Charity

All humans have faults. God allows just enough idiosyncrasies and shortcomings to teach people humility, temper their egos and allow them to practice patience and charity. True love is to do what a person can to help another reach Heaven.

Assist others whenever possible. Encourage, charitably guide and help those in need. Pray for all, including those who have drifted, realizing they can still return by means of God's grace.

Charity must be practiced at all times and in all places despite conflicting mannerisms and clashing personalities. Charity helps remove friction from relationships. This is especially important in marriage where day-to-day situations need the balm of charity to preserve love and domestic tranquility.

Difference Between the Emotion and the Will

There is a vast difference between emotions and will. Emotions go up and down like a roller coaster while the will can remain firm. Although someone may have suffered an injury from another, a person should never retain hatred in the heart.

Forgive and move on, even though an emotional hurt may remain. Forgiveness makes one Christlike and raises a person above mere emotions. Christ will generously reward even a glass of cold water given in charity.

St. Paul said to be kind to everyone. "If it be possible, as far as in you lies, be at peace with all."[152] Being charitable isn't always easy and no one can please everyone, yet this virtue raises one to a supernatural level.

Even saints have rough edges. There were even personality clashes between some Apostles and disciples and St. Paul related the conflict between Evodia and Syntche.[153] Since people view things differently, one needs to be patient and considerate in spite of personal feelings when dealing with others.

Although Jesus on the Cross could have cast His enemies into Hell, He instead asked His Father to forgive them. Archbishop Luis Martinez in his book *The Sanctifier* says "...we have to love the good and the bad, friends and enemies. Charity does not admit exceptions."[154]

Charity for All

Love of neighbor encompasses all human beings since they were created by Almighty God and redeemed by the Precious Blood of Jesus. Christians should assist one other, raise those who fall, encourage the desolate, comfort the sorrowful, and pray for the living and the dead.

Faith and hearing are often the last things to leave the dying. Those with dementia and Alzheimer's often retain a remembrance of their faith in spite of their condition and the Rosary, scapular, act of contrition, prayers, and sacramentals give them great consolation.

Look Below the Surface

Although people often see only the exterior, God reads the heart. People are like icebergs, there is often much more below than appears on the surface.

In your dealings with others, don't always take things at face value. There is often an entirely different side that hasn't been explored. Those viewing the ocean from above see only whitecaps and azure waves. Divers see an amazing world just a few feet below.

My sister used to ride a bike in college to commute about the campus. Although she used various locks and chains, bikes kept getting stolen.

A friend found an easy way to prevent this occurrence by spray painting the bike an ugly green and covering the handlebars with black electrical tape. Its appearance was such that she often kept it unlocked. *No one* ever attempted to steal it, even though it was *exactly* like other bikes stolen from the same rack. People were even ashamed to ride it.

What's in It for Me?

When tempted to complain about the sacrifices needed to preserve mutual charity, remember that Heaven's gatekeeper, St. Peter, says, "...charity covers a multitude of sins."[155] St. James relates one's eternal salvation is nearly assured if a person helps another save his soul. "...He who causes a sinner to be brought back from his misguided way will save his soul... and will cover a multitude of sins."[156]

---

[152] Romans 12, 18.
[153] 1 Philippians 4, 2.
[154] pp. 243-244.
[155] 1 Peter 4, 8.
[156] James 5, 20.

Those who practice charity will have a great reward in Heaven. "...as long as you did it for one of these, the least of My brethren, you did it for Me."[157] "Practicing charity" is not a one-time event, but encompasses a lifetime.

Grace transforms a person, enabling him to practice virtue and eradicate evil habits. He becomes dear to God and God becomes very dear to him.

Prayer is no longer viewed as a burden, but rather becomes an opportunity to speak with God, thank Him and ask for assistance. Confidence soars because of the close relationship with God.

Heidi and *Exidor*

Mount Saint Michael in Spokane, Washington was once home to two German Shepherds. Everyone loved *Heidi,* a model of gentleness who followed my mom to the chapel and mailbox. *Exidor* was an attack dog from a police canine unit and a feature at a haunted house. Once when walking outside the seminary I heard yelps and saw *Exidor* wrapped in his chain.

At first I thought, *he deserves it*, and began to walk away. Then something told me to help the helpless dog. I looked *Exidor* in the eye and said, "You better be good." I then untied the tethered animal. *Exidor* then began to lick me and we remained friends for life.

Charity in Action

I received an email from a friend in Japan describing her visit to her dying cousin. Since he wasn't Catholic, she gently explained to him the basics of the Faith and showed him a crucifix and pictures of Jesus and Mary. She calmly let him decide for himself, but kept praying for God to assist him. Masses were offered for his conversion as well.

After a couple hours, he manifested his wish to be baptized and took the name of Joseph. After receiving Baptism, he closed his eyes, and the tear of joy that followed convinced her the Catholic Faith had given him peace of mind. He died tranquilly two days later.

Good example draws others closer to God. The lady's father was converted years earlier by the good example of Catholics when he worked at a convent as a handyman. St. Francis of Assisi described the importance of good example when he said to preach the Gospel always and only use words when necessary.

Cardinal Virtues

St. Catherine of Siena says "charity gives life to all the virtues."[158] These include the cardinal[159] virtues of Prudence, Justice, Fortitude, and Temperance. The cardinal virtues moderate and balance the life of a Catholic in order to prevent the two extremes of laxity and rigorism. Self-love destroys charity and affection towards one's neighbor and is the principle and foundation of every evil.[160]

One of the greatest consolations at Judgment will be the practice of charity and the remembrance of defending God's honor and law. His champions, who remained faithful and endured ridicule and persecution for His sake, will merit a high place in Heaven.

---

[157] Matthew 25, 40.
[158] *Dialogue.*
[159] The word *cardinal* is derived from the Latin word for *hinge* since many other virtues are related to them.
[160] See St. Catherine of Siena, *Dialogue.*

Chapter Fourteen

Temptation

The final words of the Lord's Prayer are, "...lead us not into temptation, but deliver us from evil. Amen." These petitions ask for help to overcome temptation and are a reminder to avoid *occasions of sin—persons, places and things that lead one away from God.* Jesus counseled the Apostles to "watch and pray that you may not enter into temptation."[161]

Temptation is a Test and there are Three Courses of Action Possible

1) *Resisting temptation* is like keeping the door of one's heart closed.

2) *Partial consent* is listening to temptation, but not giving in completely.

The door of the heart opens, but only partially. The safety chain remains attached.

3) *Full consent* is knowingly & willingly performing a sinful action. The door is wide open.

Three Enemies

Humans are attacked by three foes, *a corrupt world, the devil* and *fallen human nature* (concupiscence). None of these hinder the free will, but they entice one to sin by presenting it as an apparent good, something pleasing to the senses.

Some sins are due to weakness, others to malice (an evil intention). It is necessary to gain control over temptations since sinful habits can easily control a person's life.

Demons veil the evil nature of sin and its long-term consequences. They make it appear as something desirable that everyone does. In reality, all the devils can do is offer counterfeits—short-term, sinful pleasure in place of lasting happiness. The two are worlds apart.

Sinful pleasure only causes remorse since men and women were created by and for God. Therefore, as St. Augustine says, the human heart remains restless, until it rests in the Lord.

Years of Experience

Demons have centuries of experience and lead many astray. St. Bernard reminds individuals that devils succeeded in deceiving those advanced in virtue who abandoned prayer or were too reliant on their own strength including wise Solomon, holy King David and mighty Samson. Most falls are caused by pride. Since devils sense the weakness of people by observing them, they form custom-made temptations adapted to each individual.

Close the Door Immediately

Devils can attack like a roaring lion or a stealthy assassin. Once the door is open, it becomes difficult to close. Demons often resemble telemarketers who offer something a person doesn't want. Don't listen! Hang up. Resist temptations immediately.

St. Paul writes, "God is faithful and will not permit you to be tempted beyond your strength, but with the temptation will also give you a way out that you may be able to bear it."[162]

---

[161] Matthew 26, 41.
[162] 1 Corinthians 10, 12-13.

Hidden Traps

Devils are deceivers, liars and counterfeiters who try to convince people to avoid church, the Mass and sacraments, and give up prayer and God. Demons are jealous of others taking their place in Heaven and do their utmost to lead souls astray. Their only aim is to rob individuals of sanctifying grace so they damn their souls and suffer eternally with them in Hell.

Evil spirits never tell people that by committing a mortal sin they will lose sanctifying grace, and all merit, and will be punished forever unless they repent before death. Once a soul has fallen into serious sin it often becomes immersed in it, like one falling into quicksand. Why would anyone risk enduring an eternity of suffering for a few minutes of sinful gratification? It's just not worth it!

Demons lure people to gossip, destroy the reputations of others, steal, physically harm others, or commit sins of impurity, telling them they are special and the rules don't apply.

Don't debate with the devils. They are sly liars who attempt to lead people into sin without revealing the harmful or fatal consequences of evil actions. St. Peter says to:

> Be sober, be watchful for your adversary the devil, as a roaring lion, goes about seeking someone to devour. Resist him, steadfast in the faith, knowing that the same suffering befalls your brethren all over the world.[163]

Devils craftily lead some to *presumption,* telling them to go ahead and sin because they can always go to confession later. Others are lead to *despair* and told the situation is hopeless, that they will never change or that God will never forgive them.

Although Jesus died to redeem each individual and will never reject anyone who asks for forgiveness and wants to return to His love, no one is assured of having the opportunity to repent before death.

Weakness Transformed into Strength

St. Paul advises all to "take up the armor of God that you may be able to resist in the evil day."[164] God will always assist a person to overcome temptation if he or she prays for help.

By triumphing over temptation, one becomes spiritually stronger. By remaining humble, a person grows in love of God and the bond between the soul and God deepens. Gold is purified by fire. Steel gains strength through compression and pruned trees produce better fruit.

Virtue is acquired by repeated acts. Temptations overcome and trials patiently borne transform carbon (human nature) into diamonds (saints who earn eternal happiness).

God draws good out of evil. By persevering in prayer and renouncing occasions of sin, saints see life as it really is and merit the eternal happiness of Heaven. By the grace of God they achieve a degree of holiness that would be otherwise humanly impossible.

Examine the lives of the saints. None was exempt from trials, temptation or persecution. They persevered and became holy by means of their difficulties. Although life appears at times to be a mystery, like the back of a tapestry, when it is flipped, a masterpiece is often revealed.

---

[163] 1 Peter 5, 8-10.
[164] Ephesians 6, 13.

Chapter Fifteen

Sin

There are two kinds of sin, *mortal* and *venial*. The *Baltimore Catechism* calls sin: "...a willful thought, word, deed, or omission forbidden by the law of God."[165] Some examples are:

Sinful Thoughts   uncharitable or impure thoughts, despair, doubts against the Faith

Sinful Words   gossip, slander, impure speech, lying

Sinful Deeds   sinful actions, causing scandal

Sinful Omission   neglecting responsibilities or prayer, Mass, or the sacraments

Venial Sin

A venial sin is a lesser offense against the law of God. The word *venial* is taken from the Latin word *venia* meaning *pardon*. Venial sins should not be taken lightly because they offend God.

Mortal Sin

Mortal sin is a serious offense against the law of God. The word *mortal* is taken from the Latin word *mors* meaning *death*. It is a deadly sin because it robs one of sanctifying grace—the ticket to Heaven. If a person dies in the state of unrepentant mortal sin, he or she will burn eternally in Hell and be forever separated from God.

St. John Chrysostom says that devils conceal the evil of sin, revealing only the enticing part that appeals to the senses and passions. Sin, hatred, dishonesty, greed, immorality, and pride bring misery here and hereafter. Sinful actions offend God, hurt the individual and negatively transform society. They also demand restitution to the justice of God.

Three Conditions Necessary for a Sin to be Mortal

1) The offense *must be serious.*
2) A person *must know the offense is serious.*
3) An individual *must give full consent of the will.*

The sin is venial if any of these three conditions is absent.

Seven Capital Sins

There are seven roots from which all sins are derived called the *Seven Capital Sins* or the *Deadly Sins.* They are *pride, anger, sloth, covetousness, lust, envy,* and *gluttony.*

Devils Try to Lead Those Leading Virtuous Lives into Sin

St. Alphonsus Liguori warned those striving for holiness to beware.

Even the saints have been tormented by temptations. The devil labors harder to make the saints fall, than to make the wicked sin: he regards the saints as more valuable prey.[166]

---

[165] p. 20.
[166] *Sermon.* See Rosemary Guiley, *The Quotable Saint,* p. 236.

The Ten Commandments

Human beings need to work within parameters. God's laws set moral boundaries in order to safeguard virtue and help eradicate vice. They insure God's honor, right order in society and concord among individuals.

Every sin is a direct attack against God and His dominion by creatures who owe Him reverence and obedience. Moses received the Ten Commandments from God on Mt. Sinai around the year 1500 BC. They are a specific set of laws given by God to direct all on how to live.

God engraved these precise laws on tablets of stone to show they were permanent commands that were not to be arbitrarily changed as time passed.

The Ten Commandments are not to be taken lightly. If a person faithfully follows them, he will save his soul. Those who disregard them will lose their soul.

God loves everyone since He created each individual, but He also expects everyone to follow His rules—the Ten Commandments. Our Lord said, "If you love Me, keep My commandments."[167] If society is not indifferent about behavior and punishes malefactors, is not God entitled to do the same?

If a person is truly sorry and repentant, God will pardon sin through the Sacrament of Penance and restore sanctifying grace to the soul of one who returns to Him. Christ gives priests and bishops power to forgive sins since they continue His mission on earth.

Over the centuries many have sinfully misused their five senses for self-gratification. Misuse does not make the body or senses evil in themselves. God in His justice will severely punish those who view illicit objects (sight), listen to gossip and impure stories (hearing), engage in gluttony, drug or alcohol abuse (taste), or commit impure actions (touch).

---

[167] John 14, 15.

Chapter Sixteen

The First Commandment

"I am the Lord thy God, thou shalt not have strange gods before Me."   Exodus 20, 2-3

Although the First and Third Commandments appear to be very different, there are surprisingly many similarities. Since God created humans, He has certain rights over them and they have corresponding responsibilities, including to love and honor Him.

All have an obligation in justice to obey His commandments, be baptized, become members of the Catholic Church that Jesus founded, practice the Faith, pray daily, and assist at Mass on all Sundays and Holy Days of Obligation.

Sins Against Faith

The First Commandment forbids joining other religions and actively participating in non-Catholic rituals. The *Baltimore Catechism* says "a Catholic sins against faith by taking part in non-Catholic worship because he thus professes belief in a religion he knows is false."[168] The Bible is very clear: "Thou shalt not adore their gods nor serve them."[169] "The Lord thy God shalt thou worship and Him only shalt thou serve."[170]

Jesus Christ, Who founded the Catholic Church, the one, true Church, said: "He who believes and is baptized shall be saved, but he who does not believe shall be condemned."[171] St. John spoke in a similar manner. "If anyone comes to you and does not bring this doctrine, do not receive him into the house, or say to him, Welcome."[172]

There are over 26,000 Christian churches and 4,000 different religions in the world today. All have different beliefs, worship and teachings. Therefore, the Catholic Church teaches that: "It is unlawful for the faithful [Catholics] to assist in any active manner, or to take part in the sacred services of non-Catholics."[173]

Active participation in non-Catholic worship, called *communicatio in sacris,* includes joining in formal prayers and worship, going to communion in non-Catholic churches and similar actions. Popes Pius IX, St. Pius X, Pius XI, and Pius XII condemned these practices.

A person may attend weddings and funerals in non-Catholic churches as long as he doesn't participate and there is no danger to one's faith. The wedding should be the first marriage for each party unless they are otherwise eligible to be married in God's eyes (i.e. widowed). Out of respect, those attending should stand and sit with others in the congregation.

The First Commandment forbids consulting fortune-tellers, reading horoscopes, practicing superstition, reading tarot cards, and similar activities. Ouija Boards are extremely dangerous and often lead to diabolical possession. Since only God knows the future, it shows lack of trust in Him to turn to others who merely guess or fraudulently claim to predict upcoming events.

---

[168] Fr. Francis Connell, *Baltimore Catechism No. 3*, p. 124.
[169] Exodus 22, 24.
[170] Matthew 4, 10.
[171] Mark 16, 16.
[172] 2 John 1, 10.
[173] Canon 1258.

Heresy, Apostasy and Schism

Heresy is a rejection of one or more *de fide* teachings of the Catholic Church. *Heresy* is derived from the Greek word for *choice*. Well-known heretics include Arius, Calvin, Luther, and Cranmer. Canon Law defines a heretic as:

> ...one who after Baptism, while remaining nominally a Christian, pertinaciously [with conscious and intentional resistance to the authority of God and the Church] denies or doubts any of the truths which must be believed of divine and Catholic Faith.[174]

Apostasy occurs when a baptized Catholic gives up the practice of the Faith. Apostasy is so prevalent today that it is being called the Post-Christian Era. Two infamous apostates include Julian the Apostate and Queen Elizabeth I of England.

Schism occurs when "a baptized person... rejects the authority of the Supreme Pontiff or refuses Communion with members of the Church who are subject to him."[175] *Schism* is derived from the Greek word for *division*. Schismatics deny papal primacy and papal infallibility, both infallible dogmas of the Catholic Church. *Papal primacy* means the pope is above all other bishops and exercises universal jurisdiction over the entire Church. *Papal infallibility* means the pope cannot err when teaching the universal Church in matters of faith and morals.

The Importance of Fervent Prayer

During the winter of 1812, Napoleon's troops marched across Germany. A farm family whose home was in the path of the advancing French Army prayed to God for protection. The devout grandmother repeated the prayer, "Build Thou a wall around us that the enemy may not approach our habitation." She knew they needed help and that God would answer her prayers.

A violent wintry storm arose during the night that formed huge snowdrifts completely concealing the farmhouse from view. Although French soldiers marched right past the farm for two consecutive days they never even realized it was there. God doesn't always work similar miracles, but He always hears prayers and rewards fidelity.

---

[174] Canon 1325.
[175] Canon 1325.

Chapter Seventeen

The Third Commandment

The Third Commandment obliges one to worship God and refrain from performing unnecessary servile work on Sunday. Exodus 20, 8 mandates "Remember that thou keep holy the Sabbath." Deuteronomy 5, 12 says "Observe the day of the Sabbath, to sanctify it, as the Lord thy God hath commanded thee."

Catholics sanctify the Sabbath[176] by attending the Holy Sacrifice of the Mass on every Sunday and Holy Day of Obligation. This serious duty is also a Law of the Church. Christ performed a number of miracles on the Sabbath in order to show He came to establish the New Law.

The Sabbath is a day consecrated to God and set aside for people to adore Him, get needed rest and briefly put aside their normal daily activities.

People are not to do unnecessary manual labor (servile work) or unnecessary shopping on Sundays. The Church transferred the Sabbath from Saturday to Sunday to commemorate Christ's Resurrection and the Descent of the Holy Ghost at Pentecost which occurred on Sundays. Necessary occupations on Sunday include: Mass attendance, cooking, acts of charity, etc. Sports, hobbies and activities that engage the mind more than the body are allowed.

The Holy Sacrifice of the Mass

The Passion, Death and Resurrection of Our Lord are the greatest events that have ever occurred on earth. Jesus instituted the Mass in order to renew in an unbloody manner the Sacrifice of the Cross and dispense the copious graces merited by His sufferings.

The Mass is a sacrifice, a word that literally means *offering something holy to God*. Christ offers the Mass through the priest since He is the Sacrificial Victim glorifying and appeasing Almighty God. The vestments, ceremonies and prayers reflect on the Passion, Resurrection and Ascension of Christ. The Holy Sacrifice of the Mass is the greatest of all prayers. The sacrificial character of the Mass is shown in the Offertory, Consecration and Communion.

The Three Essential Parts of the Mass

Offertory   bread and wine are offered to God

Consecration   bread and wine are changed into the Body, Blood, Soul, and Divinity of Christ

Communion   individuals receive Jesus in the Sacred Host

One does not fulfill the requirement of attending Mass on a Sunday or Holy Day of Obligation if he or she misses a notable part of the Mass. If a person misses one of the three major parts of the Mass on a Sunday or Holy Day of Obligation, he or she must make up that part at a subsequent Mass provided one is present for both the Consecration and Communion of the same Mass.[177]

Being habitually late for Mass indicates a weak faith. It distracts those in attendance and shows a lack of respect for God and others. It is a venial sin to be purposely late for Mass.

---

[176] Sabbath is a Hebrew word for day of rest.
[177] *Baltimore Catechism #3*, q. 237, p. 139.

The Holy Sacrifice of the Mass and the Passion of Christ

The ceremonies of the Holy Sacrifice of the Mass represent the various events that took place during Christ's Passion, Death and Resurrection.

The Priest goes to the Altar Jesus goes to the Garden of Gethsemane.

Prayers at the Foot of the Altar Christ foresees His terrible sufferings and the sins of the world causing Him to sweat blood. Jesus perseveres in prayer while His Apostles sleep.

The Priest kisses the Altar Our Lord is betrayed by Judas' kiss.

Introit Jesus is brought before Annas and is struck by one of the attendants.

Kyrie Eleison St. Peter denies Our Lord three times. (The *Kyrie* is recited in Greek.)

Gloria Christ is brought before the high priest Caiphas.

Dominus Vobiscum Jesus gazes at Peter after his denials.

Epistle Christ is led to the Roman Governor, Pontius Pilate and accused by false witnesses.

Gospel King Herod mocks Our Lord.

Creed The soldiers and crowd insult Christ.

Offertory Our Redeemer is scourged and crowned with thorns.

Washing of the Hands Pontius Pilate washes his hands.

Orate Fratres Our Lord is presented before the people.

Preface / Sanctus Jesus is condemned to death while the crowd cries, "Crucify Him!"

Canon of the Mass Christ carries the Cross, is met by His Blessed Mother and falls several times. Veronica wipes the Sacred Face of Jesus.

Hanc Igitur When Jesus arrives on Calvary, He is stripped of His garments and crucified.

Quam Oblationem Our Lord is nailed to the Cross.

Consecration The priest reenacts the miracle of the Last Supper when he, in the person of Christ, repeats the words and actions of Our Lord whereby the substance of the bread and wine are changed into the Body, Blood, Soul, and Divinity of Jesus Christ. This miracle is called Transubstantiation. The separate consecrations of the host and wine represent the Sacrifice of Christ shedding His Blood for our redemption and dying on the Cross.

Elevation Our Lord is raised on the Cross and His Precious Blood flows from His wounds.

Last Prayers of the Canon / Our Father The Seven Last Words of Christ from the Cross.

The Host is Broken Our Redeemer dies upon the Cross.

A Particle of the Host is placed in the Chalice Our Lord's Sacred Body is taken down from the Cross and His soul descends into Limbo.

Agnus Dei The Roman centurion, St. Longinus pierces Christ's Sacred Heart with a lance.

Priest's Communion / The Communion of the Faithful Jesus is laid in the tomb.

Prayers after Communion Our Lord rises from the dead.

Ite Missa Est Jesus ascends into Heaven.

The Priest Gives his Blessing The Descent of the Holy Ghost at Pentecost.

Last Gospel The Gospel is preached throughout the world.

Ancient Languages and the Rites in the Church

Christ taught the Apostles how to offer Mass in the ancient Hebrew tongue also known as Aramaic[178] or Old Chaldean. The various rites of the Catholic Church, formed as the Apostles evangelized the world, have used vernacular languages in their liturgies for centuries.

The Holy Sacrifice of the Mass is still offered throughout the world in Latin, the language used in the Roman Empire. Latin, which dates to the sixth century BC, ceased to be a spoken language between the seventh and eighth centuries. Through the course of time, it and other languages used for Mass were no longer spoken, yet were retained in order to preserve the liturgical integrity.

Many localized liturgies emerged in the early ages of the Church since travel was difficult, books rare, and communication primitive. Persecutions enhanced the difficulties. In spite of minor differences, Eastern and Western liturgies historically were substantially the same and contained the three essential elements of Offertory, Consecration and Communion.

Eastern Rites of the Catholic Church[179]

Alexandrian	Catholic Coptics (Egyptian), Ethiopian Catholics (Abyssinian)
Syrian (Antiochian)	Maronite, Syrians
Armenian	Catholic Armenians
Greek (Byzantine)	Albanian, Bulgarian, Georgian, Greek Catholics, Hungarian, Melkite, Italo-Greeks, Rumanian, Ruthenian, Russian Catholics, Serbian
Chaldean	Chaldeans, Malabar Catholics

A number of Eastern European and Asian churches used the Liturgy of St. James. Churches in Palestine, Syria and North Africa utilized the Liturgy of St. Mark. Most of Western Europe adopted the Liturgy of St. Peter, known today as the Latin Rite.

Western Rites of the Catholic Church

Latin	The Latin Mass dates back to at least 150 AD[180]
Ambrosian	Milan, Italy
Mozarabic	Toledo, Spain

Following the Council of Trent (1545-1563), the Celtic (Ireland), Lyonese and Gallican (France) Rites of the Church joined the Latin Rite. They adopted the *Missale Romanum* and offered the Tridentine Latin Mass.

Graces Received from Devout Attendance at Mass

St. Augustine relates many singular graces derived from Mass attendance.

> He who devoutly hears holy Mass will receive a great vigor to enable him to resist mortal sin, and there shall be pardoned to him all venial sins which he may have committed up to that hour.[181]

---

[178] See Eric North, *Book of a Thousand Tongues*, p. 19.
[179] Many Orthodox (schismatic churches) that deny papal primacy comd other dogmas have similar names.
[180] See the writings of St. Justin and St. Hippolytus (215 AD). The Latin Mass was offered widely in the Roman Empire in 250 AD.
[181] Sup. Can. Quia passus, de Consecr. dist. 2.

Devout attendance at Mass draws down so many benefits that St. Leonard of Port Maurice calls it the golden key of paradise.[182] These include—temporal blessings, protection from natural disasters, blessings on one's work, final perseverance, and leading sinners to penitence.

St. Anselm encourages Catholics to attend Mass whenever possible since one Mass attended or offered for a person during life is more efficacious than 1,000 celebrated after one's death.[183]

The Holy Sacrifice of the Mass is a renewal in an unbloody manner of the Sacrifice of Jesus on the Cross. At each Mass, Christ mystically renews His Passion, pleads for mercy on the human race and bestows God's choicest graces upon those attending.

Symbolism of Objects in Church

The main altar in a Catholic church customarily faces east. On top of the altar is the **tabernacle**, [184] an ornate brass safe draped with a silk veil. It protects the consecrated Hosts that are stored in the **ciborium**.[185]

Three linen altar cloths cover the top of the altar. *Linen* is used because it is highly absorbent. Beneath the cloths is an **altar stone**, a piece of marble with five engraved crosses that commemorate Jesus' wounds. Each altar stone contains relics of two martyrs that the priest reverently kisses during Mass.

Two Low Mass **candles** flank the tabernacle while six High Mass candles rest on a **gradine** (shelf) at the back of the altar. The wick and wax of beeswax candles[186] represent the two natures of Jesus—divine and human. The flame symbolizes Christ, the Light of the World. Beeswax, formed by virginal bees, recalls the virginal birth of Jesus. There was also a practical aspect for their use since candles supplied light for Mass.

Three **altar cards** contain prayers said by the priest during Mass. The right card has prayers said at the Washing of the Hands and the left one has the Last Gospel. The center card has the Gloria, Prayer before the Gospel, the Credo, Offertory Prayers, the Words of Consecration, Prayers to the Blessed Trinity, and three prayers recited before the priest's communion.

Resting on the top, or suspended above the tabernacle, is the **crucifix** that recalls to both priest and laity the close relationship between the Holy Sacrifice of the Mass and Jesus' Passion and Death on Calvary.

To the left of the tabernacle or suspended above the sanctuary is a red glass **sanctuary lamp**. The burning candle inside reminds the faithful that Jesus is present in the tabernacle.

The **Missale Romanum**[187] Latin missal rests on the **missal stand** on the epistle (right) side of the altar. It contains the prayers recited by the priest during Mass.

Statues in niches, above side altars and in various places in church remind one that saints who lived on earth now reign in Heaven and intercede for the faithful.

---

[182] *The Hidden Treasure: Holy Mass,* p. 40.
[183] Apud Castell, diur. sac. Praep.
[184] Hebrew word for *tent* that recalls the Holy of Holies in the Old Testament.
[185] A gold plated silver vessel with a lid. Ciborium in Latin means a *container of food.*
[186] Candles in U.S. churches are allowed to be 51% beeswax due to the high cost of 100% beeswax candles.
[187] The Roman Missal dates back to 1570, just after the Council of Trent. It is, therefore, called the Tridentine Latin Mass.

Stained glass windows portray images of God, the Blessed Virgin, saints, angels, Gospel scenes, the mysteries of the Rosary, and other edifying topics. They help the faithful rise above the mundane and focus on the supernatural mysteries of Faith.

The **cruet** (credence) **table** holds items necessary for Mass including glass or crystal wine and water **cruets**, the lavabo dish, finger towel, bells, and communion paten.

A glass or crystal dish with a lid called the **ablution bowl** rests upon the **altar gradine** and is used by the priest to purify his fingers when Holy Communion is distributed outside of Mass.

The **communion rail** separates the **sanctuary** (apse) from the **nave** (body) of the church. At communion time a linen cloth is placed over the communion rail in order to retrieve the Host in case It accidentally falls from the priest's hand during the distribution of Holy Communion.

Fourteen Stations of the Cross, mounted on the sidewalls of a church, recall the sufferings of Jesus. They are used to assist those who pray the devotion, especially during Lent.

Relics of saints are often found resting on the altar gradine in decorative reliquaries. **Flowers** are used on the main and side altars to beautify the House of God.

The faithful customarily make the Sign of the Cross with **holy water** from **fonts** located near the doors of a church upon entering. Catholics reverently **genuflect** on the right knee when entering or leaving church in order to show respect for Jesus in the tabernacle. This is believed to be a chivalrous custom begun by St. Francis of Assisi.

It has been a custom since the time of St. Paul[188] for women to wear **head coverings** in church. These can be ornate and decorative. Many women and girls prefer Spanish style mantillas because they are graceful and dignified, and show reverence for God.

The Liturgical Year

As the four seasons with their special characteristics enliven daily life, the liturgical year and sanctoral cycle likewise inspire Catholics by their focus on the various aspects of Christ's life and with a variety of feasts honoring Our Lady, the saints and angels.

The Church year begins with the liturgical season of **Advent**,[189] the four Sundays preceding Christmas.

Christmas, the feast commemorating Jesus' Birth, is observed on December 25. A week later, the feast of the Circumcision of Our Lord, is held on January 1.

January 6 is the feast of the **Epiphany**.[190] It focuses on Christ's manifestation to the world typified by the visit of the Three Kings to Bethlehem, the manifestation of the Blessed Trinity at Jesus' Baptism in the Jordan River and Our Lord's first public miracle, the changing of water into wine at the Marriage of Cana.

---

[188] See 1 Corinthians 5, 10.
[189] From the Latin word for *coming*.
[190] From the Greek word for *manifestation*.

The transitional season between Epiphany and Lent called **Septuagesima** includes Septuagesima, [191] Sexagesima [192] and Quinquagesima [193] Sundays. Even though violet vestments are used, flowers may be placed on the altar and the organ may be played at Mass.

The 40-day season of **Lent**[194] begins on Ash Wednesday. This penitential season recalls Jesus' 40-day fast in the desert.[195]

The last two weeks of Lent called **Passiontide** include Passion Sunday (when the statues are covered with purple veils), the feast of the Seven Dolors of Mary (Friday before Good Friday), Palm Sunday (when palms are blessed and distributed), and Holy Week.

The date of **Easter**, the greatest feast of the Church year, changes annually because it is always held on the first Sunday after the Paschal Full Moon.

The number of Sundays after Epiphany, Easter and Pentecost vary according to the date of Easter. The Sunday following Ascension Thursday commemorates Christ's Ascension.

The Feast of **Pentecost**, the birthday of the Catholic Church, is celebrated 50 days after Easter. It commemorates the Descent of the Holy Ghost upon Mary and the Apostles.

The Sunday immediately following Pentecost is called Trinity Sunday and honors One God in Three Divine Persons–Father, Son and Holy Ghost. The remainder of the Sundays of the year are called **Sundays after Pentecost**.

Vestment Colors

Violet   The color of vestments worn during Advent, Lent, Passiontide, Septuagesima, most Ember Days, Rogation Days, and Vigils

Green   Sundays after Epiphany and Pentecost

White   Feasts of Our Lord, Our Lady, Angels, and Saints who were not Martyrs and during Nuptial (wedding) Masses

Red   Pentecost week, Masses of the Holy Ghost, Holy Cross and Passion, feasts of Martyrs (men, women and children who shed their blood for Christ)

Gold   May be used in place of white, red and green; often used on Christmas, Easter and other major feasts

Rose   Third Sunday of Advent and the Fourth Sunday of Lent

Black   Requiem Masses (offered for the Faithful Departed) and funerals

Spiritual Communion

There are times when a person is unable to receive Holy Communion due to not fulfilling the communion fast[196] or when responsibilities prevent a person from attending Mass. Saints and

---

[191] From the Latin word for *70*.
[192] From the Latin word for *60*.
[193] From the Latin word for *50*.
[194] From the Anglo-Saxon word meaning *spring*.
[195] For more information on fasting, see Chapter 38.
[196] See p. 88 for specifics.

spiritual writers encourage *spiritual communion* whereby one asks Jesus to enter his heart and soul in a spiritual manner by saying, "Dear Jesus, please come spiritually into my heart."

The person should then speak to Our Lord and make acts of adoration, love, desire, trust, contrition, and thanksgiving. One may also ask for special graces to become patient and charitable and to persevere in the grace of God. Many benefits are derived from this pious practice that helps one achieve a closer union with God.

The Church Calendar

The Proper of the Saints in the Church calendar begins on November 29 with St. Saturninus, bishop and martyr from Toulouse, France and ends on November 26, St. Sylvester, the abbot.

Saints have come from every era and every region of the world. Although these holy men and women were often persecuted, everything will be different during the Last Judgment as described in the Book of Wisdom 5, 5. "We fools esteemed their life madness and their end without honor, behold how they are numbered among the children of God and their lot is among the saints."

Holydays of Obligation

Holydays of obligation vary according to country. Those observed in the United States are:

Christmas	(December 25)	**Assumption of Mary**	(August 15)
Circumcision of Our Lord	(January 1)	**All Saints' Day**	(November 1)
Ascension Thursday	(40 days after Easter)	**Immaculate Conception**	(December 8)

Vigils

A vigil is the day preceding an important feast. The two current privileged vigils include those of Christmas and Pentecost. Holy Saturday ceremonies are called the Easter Vigil.

Common vigils are the days preceding the feasts of the Ascension, Immaculate Conception, Assumption, St. John the Baptist, St. Lawrence, and the Apostles Peter and Paul. The Vigils of the Immaculate Conception, Christmas and Easter are days of fast and complete abstinence. The Vigil of Pentecost is a day of fast and partial abstinence. There is no fasting or abstinence on the other vigils. They have been retained to draw attention to important feasts.

Rogation Days

Rogation Days[197] appease God's wrath, petition Him to avert calamities and ask His blessings upon the crops. St. Gregory the Great (598 AD) introduced the Major Rogation Day that is observed on April 25, the feast of St. Mark. St. Mamertus, bishop of Vienne (470 AD) established the Minor Rogation Days, the three days preceding Ascension Thursday.

The Litany of the Saints is customarily prayed in procession or in church by the clergy and faithful on Rogation Days. To add solemnity, a server leads the procession swinging a *thurible*, an incense burner that symbolizes prayers ascending to God. He is followed by a cross bearer, torchbearers, clergy, and laity.

---

[197] Derived from the Latin word *to ask*.

Ember Days

The Catholic Church established Ember Days to show gratitude to God for His blessings, to pray for those who were going to be ordained priests, and to revive one's spiritual life by prayer, fasting and abstinence. The Ember Days are the Wednesday, Friday and Saturday following December 13 (the Feast of St. Lucy), the First Sunday of Lent, September 14 (the Exaltation of the Holy Cross), and Pentecost Sunday. There is one set of Ember Days in each season—winter, spring, summer, and fall.

Ordinations often occur during Ember Days. The Wednesday and Saturday of these weeks are days of fast and partial abstinence. Friday is a day of fast and total abstinence.

The liturgical year demonstrates that the Catholic Church is both ancient and new, having the oldest consistent form of worship on Earth. The Latin, Greek and Aramaic used in the Tridentine Latin Mass reflect the Church's antiquity and adaptation to every time and age.

Chapter Eighteen

The Second Commandment

"Thou shalt not take the name of the Lord thy God in vain."   Exodus 20, 7

The name of God was so sacred in Old Testament times that people were forbidden from ever saying it and the Our Father contains the words, "hallowed be Thy name." Today the name of God is more frequently used to express anger, surprise or wonder than in devout prayer. What caused this tragic transformation?

Those who despised God throughout history often used His name in derision or in curses. Since people often imitate what they hear, today this practice has become so commonplace that many use God's name in an irreverent manner without even thinking about it.

Respecting God's Name

The Second Commandment condemns irreverent use of the name of God and Jesus. God's name should be treated with reverence, never spoken in anger, in blasphemy, or to curse a person, place or thing. The words uttered from one's lips reflect what resides in the heart.

Rubrics command priests to respectfully bow their head at the name of Jesus during Mass. It is a pious practice for Catholics to bow their head when the Holy Name of Jesus is said or heard.

The Second Commandment commends lawful vows (marriage vows, religious vows and others) and oaths such as those in courts of law.

Dishonoring God

God is all-powerful and infinite. Blasphemous utterances and using God's name inappropriately will not go unpunished. St. Paul warns, "Be not deceived, God is not mocked."[198] "It is a fearful thing to fall into the hands of the living God."[199]

God does not take the matter lightly. The *Catechism of the Council of Trent* speaks of "Those so blinded by the darkness of error as not to dread to blaspheme His name, Whom the Angels glorify... shamelessly and daringly outraging His divine Majesty every day..."[200]

It is lamentable that many blasphemously ridicule God even though He provides their daily needs. Blasphemy mocks and taunts God and manifests disrespect and hatred.

The practice of using God's name in vain brings down many calamities. Scripture foretold universal disturbances in nature in the latter times. Is it any wonder that they are on the rise?

Bad Habits

If an individual frequently uses God's name in vain, that person can change a bad habit into a good one by replacing "damn it" with the words "help me" or something similar. In a short time prayer can replace swearing. Instead of becoming angry at adversity, one can learn to invoke God's assistance in time of need.

---

[198] Galatians 6, 7.
[199] Hebrews 10, 31.
[200] p. 382.

The phrase, "Oh my God," (OMG) are the first words of the Act of Contrition. These words should *only* be used reverently in prayer. Many today thoughtlessly use the phrase to express surprise or anger and often don't even realize what they are saying.

The commonly used phrase, "I swear to God," should not be used lightly. An oath petitions God to verify the truth of what one says.

A good way to prevent people from misusing God's name is to say, "blessed be God," when His name is used irreverently. If the opportunity presents itself and the individual is open minded, charitably tell the person that it is wrong to use God's name disrespectfully. Our Lord will acknowledge before His Heavenly Father on Judgment Day all those who defended His honor.

Perjury

Perjury, lying under oath, is a mortal sin. God sometimes even punishes this sin in this life. A man from Schwarstein, Germany, who lied under oath and was acquitted of stealing, wanted to "clear his name." In the courtroom he requested that a thunderbolt strike him if he was guilty. Within a week, a bolt of lightning killed him and incinerated his home.

Calling on the Names of God and Jesus

There are numerous references to the name of God and the Holy Name of Jesus in Scripture. "For whoever shall call upon the name of the Lord shall be saved."[201] "...at the name of Jesus every knee should bend of those in Heaven, on earth and under the earth [Hell]...[202] How many perils have been averted and temptations overcome by use of the name of God and Jesus!

God deserves love and respect. Developing a close relationship with God draws down blessings. David writes, "Bless the Lord, O my soul, and never forget all He has done for thee."[203]

God's Revenge

A misguided youth in Toulouse, France once defiantly pointed a dagger to the sky and blasphemously challenged God to kill him instantly if He really existed. Nothing happened at first. Then a brilliant white leaf floated down before him with the words *Have mercy on me* written in gold letters. The unbeliever became penitent and marveled at God's mercy. Once he came to realize God's infinite love, his former hatred was replaced by humble gratitude.

The best way to show gratitude for God's gifts is by leading a good life, thanking Him and loving Him. "...what hast thou that thou hast not received?"[204] St. Thomas Aquinas teaches that gratitude is shown by:

> 1) Recognition of the favor given
>
> 2) Expression of appreciation and thanks
>
> 3) Attempt to repay the favor

---

[201] Romans 10, 13.
[202] Philippians 2, 10.
[203] Psalm 102.
[204] 1 Corinthians 4, 7.

Chapter Nineteen

The Fourth Commandment

"Honor thy father and thy mother, as the Lord thy God hath commanded thee, that thou mayest live a long time, and it may be well with thee in the land, which the Lord will give thee." Deuteronomy 5, 16

Obedience, Love and Respect

After showing God the honor and respect due to His infinite majesty by the first three commandments, the Fourth Commandment describes the obligations individuals have to those on whom ones' very existence depended—a person's parents. Every individual owes their life to their father and mother, whose union at the time of conception created their body, and to God, Who at that same instant, infused an immortal soul into it.

God established marriage, the natural law contract between husband and wife, when He brought Adam and Eve together and told them to increase, multiply and fill the earth. Jesus raised the marital union to the level of a sacrament (Matrimony) in order to offer couples all the graces necessary to sanctify themselves, properly raise their children and lead them to their destiny, eternal life.

The word "honor" was chosen because the chivalrous term includes obedience, listening, respect, assistance, and in later life when necessary, support for parents. Honor is a characteristic that denotes the dignity of parents who dedicate their lives to their children. They in turn deserve love, respect, obedience, and prayers—love, put in practice.

St. Paul writes, "Children, obey your parents in all things, for that is pleasing in the Lord."[205] Children, even after leaving home, can learn from the wisdom of their parents. Respect for parents is a manifestation of love for God, whose authority they hold.

Although most children come into the world through an act of love, there are also illegitimate births, some effected by passion, others by violence. Regardless of how one entered the world, each individual is born to attain the unending joys of Heaven.

Children have the obligation to obey and respect their parents and those who helped raise them, including grandparents and relatives. Authority is also inherent in legitimate governments, law enforcement agencies, employers, clergy, principals, teachers, and others.

Of the three vows taken by Religious, the most important is obedience. It encompasses also the religious vows of chastity and poverty. Religious have a serious obligation to obey their superiors. Of Church leaders Our Lord said: "He who hears you, hears Me; and he who rejects you, rejects Me; and he who rejects Me rejects Him Who sent Me."[206]

Those in Authority Represent God

During His Passion, Jesus respected Pontius Pilate because the Roman governor's right to rule came from God. Those in positions of authority hold God's place in spite of their shortcomings. Their office must be respected. Obedience is to be shown in all matters except sin.

---

[205] Colossians 3, 20.
[206] Luke 10, 16.

Pope Leo XIII wrote: "Obedience is not servitude of man to man, but submission to the will of God, Who governs through the medium of men."[207] St. Peter said:

> Be subject to every human creature for God's sake... For such is the will of God, that by doing good you should put to silence the ignorance of foolish men. Live as freemen, yet not using your freedom as a cloak for malice but as servants of God.[208]

Disobedience to Illegitimate Authority

Those who illegitimately hold positions of power are not to be obeyed or followed. These wolves must be disobeyed and rejected, since following their commands would be detrimental to body and soul. St. Peter is recorded in the Acts of the Apostles as saying, "We ought to obey God rather than man."[209]

The Role of Parents

Parents need to realize that they must teach their children the difference between right and wrong and instill proper values. Once the children leave the home, they must lead them by good example and a life of prayer.

Although it is very discouraging to see loved ones drift, never give up. As long as there is life, there is hope. Prayer affects wonders. If God chooses not to control human beings even after creating them by bestowing the faculties of intellect and free will, parents will never be able to control all aspects of the lives of their children, especially once they leave home.

Being a parent can, at times, be a thankless job. It includes joys, sorrows, adventures, wonderful memories, special days, hard work, anxiety, numerous tears, disappointments, and restrictions on personal time and liberty. God sees all and hopefully children will remember all their parents have done on their behalf. A parent's care covers 24 hours a day until the child moves out of the home.

Parents have a serious obligation to care for, educate and lead their children to God. How could a life be called a success if someone, who excelled in the eyes of the world, lost his immortal soul? That life is a complete failure.

Obedience is greatly rewarded by God. Children must realize that they are part of a team and that mom and dad need their help in order to keep everything going and everyone happy. Chores are not punishments; they are necessary responsibilities for living at home.

King Solomon said, "My son, hear the instruction of thy father, and forsake not the law of thy mother; that grace may be added to thy head and a chain of gold to thy neck." (Proverbs 1, 8-9)

St. Gregory the Great says:

> Obedience is the only virtue which implants the other virtues in the mind and preserves them when they are implanted. Obedience is better than sacrifice: because by sacrifice the flesh of another is immolated, by obedience, our own will is sacrificed to Almighty God.[210]

Parents need to remember the words of St. Bernard. There are three ways to assist others and draw them to God—word, example and prayer, yet the greatest of these is prayer.[211]

---

[207] *Immortale Dei*, November 1, 1885.

[208] 1 Peter 2, 13, 15-16.

[209] Acts 5, 29.

[210] Very Reverend Charles Callan, OP, *Illustrations for Sermons and Instructions*, p. 274.

[211] *Manent tria haec: verbum, exemplum et oratio; major autem his est oratio.*

Pride and Rebellion

It would seem natural that children would be grateful for the countless sacrifices made on their behalf by their dedicated parents, but this is not always the case. Many children worldwide despise and dishonor their parents and some even attempt to harm and kill them. How does a person descend to such unnatural behavior?

Bad companions corrupt those around them. As good apples kept with rotten ones soon become moldy, so evil companions expose individuals to occasions and habits of sin. They teach them a myriad of bad behaviors including how to lie, cheat, steal, vandalize, dress indecently, view pornography, abuse drugs and alcohol, and lose virtue, morals, and belief in God.

Pride is the root of all sin. People don't like to be told what to do. Although most people want boundaries, especially children, many adolescents resent their parents refusing to grant them permission to do something that is sinful, harmful or imprudent.

Once Out of the House

God wants young people to develop and often start families of their own. Once a young adult moves out of the house, parents don't have the same responsibilities as previously.

Parents need to respect and support the individuality of their children and let them grow and mature into adults. Virtue is often acquired by letting them freely cooperate with God's grace and taking off the training wheels.

Parents often feel guilt regarding the lives of their children. If they had been remiss in serving as a role model, living a spiritual life, offering proper guidance and discipline when necessary, they can hopefully repair this by means of prayer, good example and prudent counsel.

Some parents believe they have been a failure and that they are somehow responsible for the wayward actions of their children. Parents have to realize that their children have free will and their actions are their own. They should not be falsely imputed to the parents.

Individuals have to want to be helped. Many learn by their mistakes. Hopefully this occurs before it's too late. Even priests can't control the lives of parishioners. Priest must try to be a good example, guide, encourage, teach, admonish, and pray for their spiritual children.

Free Will

God gives each individual the faculty of free will so a person can make decisions without coercion or force. He believed it would be better for people to merit Heaven than be given it without earning it.

Liberty can be a gift or a curse. If it is used properly, it can lead to a happy life here and eternal union with God thereafter. Misused liberty leads to sin, crime and often to Hell. Each individual is responsible for his or her actions.

Rebellion against authority leads to anarchy. Law brings needed order to society, whether it is the Ten Commandments, civil laws, ecclesiastical laws, or house rules by parents. These are an important part of God's plan.

The attitude, "no rules," leads to unhappiness and often, eternal separation from God. Rules are necessary for one's protection and are a help rather than a hindrance since they protect individual liberty and maintain harmony in society.

The Ultimate Choice

God rewards fidelity, obedience to His laws and humble submission to His will with the everlasting happiness of Heaven. Although this often entailed a sacrifice of personal liberty, saints never regretted their life of prayer and service to others, which pleases God and is a source of edification to others.

Those who lead a life of unbridled liberty, self-gratification and sinful rebellion against God and die at enmity with Him are condemned to Hell. There they are tormented by fire and eternal separation from God and confined with demons and the damned.

Ingratitude

A young man once pleaded with his mother for an early inheritance and the request was granted on condition that he support her until death. Blinded by greed, the youth hoarded the money and made his mother nearly destitute.

Realizing that the only solution was to take legal proceedings against her own son, the matron hired an attorney. Once the adolescent learned of this, he planned to kill the lawyer by purchasing a poisonous snake.

After gaining entrance into the lawyer's home, he opened the box to release the adder. Unfortunately, the viper attacked the son, leaving *him* mortally wounded. The ungrateful son quickly died after succumbing to the deadly bite.

The attorney entered his house and was puzzled to find an empty box on the floor. Soon he discovered the dead man and snake and understood what had occurred.

Chapter Twenty
The Fifth Commandment

"Thou shalt not kill."   Exodus 20, 13

Few realize the seriousness of sins of the tongue. God detests and severely punishes those who foment discord. Many will suffer the fires of Hell or Purgatory for their uncharitable speech and role in destroying the reputations of others.

Sins Against Charity in Speech and Thought

Love of God and neighbor are so intimately united that you cannot have one without the other. The relationship between an individual and God, and the bond of charity with others are essential.[212] There are many types of sins against the virtue of charity.

Hatred, like a cancer, consumes a person from within. Many act irrationally, spending their life in retaliation for supposed wrongs, or unlawfully take justice into their own hands.

Sarcasm isn't humor, but rather verbal, passive-aggressive taunting. It is a way to say an uncharitable remark without being held "accountable" because it was *only* a joke.

St. Anthony the Abbot says whisperers are more dangerous than lions, scorpions and snakes and that their mouth is filled with treachery and death. He wrote:

> All sins are less grievous than those of the *whisperer*. The *whisperer* and those who give ear to him, receive the same condemnation. ...Have no part in murmuring. For the Lord tells us that, *he that keepeth his mouth keepeth his soul*. (Proverbs 13, 3)[213]

Other Sins Against Charity

The Fifth Commandment forbids anger, impatience, taunting, uncharitable speech, bullying, hatred, fighting, causing physical harm to oneself or another, abortion, suicide, and murder. Just anger is permitted to correct abuses. Anger that gets out of control is unjust and sinful.

Self-defense is permissible. Even humble St. Francis de Sales once brandished a sword to protect his life. Taking part in just wars is permitted since a moral body has a right to protect itself and preserve its' borders.

Mortal Sins

It is a mortal sin to unjustly take the life of another, to purposely seriously injure another or commit suicide. Drinking to excess, driving while intoxicated, taking drugs without a prescription, and causing grave bodily harm to oneself or others are serious sins. These often lead to an early death and / or the deaths of others.

Never abuse drugs. Lasting effects include memory loss, impaired judgment, and when cocaine and alcohol are mixed–a heart attack. Try to work out problems rather than run from them. Turn to prayer, not to depressants. Ask God for help.

---

[212] It is an important aspect of charity to forgive injuries and pray for others.
[213] PG 40, col. 965, M. Toal, DD, *The Sunday Sermons of the Great Fathers: Volume Four*, pp. 4-5.

Suicide is never permitted. No one has the right to take his or her own life. God gives life and takes it when He is ready.

Some who commit suicide are not fully cognizant of what they are doing. God will be their judge. A person who commits suicide tragically often exchanges difficulties of this life for eternal suffering in the next and causes indescribable grief to family and friends.

Having an abortion, the deliberate murdering of a helpless child in his mother's womb, or encouraging a person to have an abortion is a mortal sin that carries the added penalty of excommunication from the Catholic Church.

Other Areas

God demands that one take reasonable care of the body, but not expose oneself to foolish risks. It is wrong to unnecessarily endanger one's own life or that of others.

When death draws near, the ordinary means of preserving life—food and fluids should not intentionally be denied to a patient. Use of extraordinary means to preserve life is optional.

Euthanasia, taking the life of another so the person can avoid pain is never permitted. People should work with their doctors to find legitimate means of controlling pain.

Remedies

One way to preserve charity is to change the subject or to leave the room when another engages in gossip or character assassination. "Talkers" should be avoided. The best way to correct the defects of others is to admonish the person in a charitable manner or pray for them.

One of the most accurate ways of gauging sanctity or lack of virtue is to examine a person's words. Those who are charitable in speech are frequently striving for perfection.[214]

---

[214] See Epistle of St. James, Chapter 3, Verse 2.

Chapter Twenty-One
The Eighth Commandment

"Thou shalt not bear false witness against thy neighbor."   Exodus 20, 16

The common phrase, "it's only a white lie" is a clear indicator of how little people value truth today. There is no such thing as a white lie. The term *white lie* is a contradiction of terms. Something is either true *or* false. Nothing can be true and false at the same time.

Lying is Detestable

The Book of Leviticus says: "Thou shalt not lie; neither shall any man deceive his neighbor."[215] St. Paul says to put away lying and be truthful.[216] Everyone has an obligation to speak the truth since lying and perjury undermine society. Lying and deceit undermine the trust needed in relationships. Nothing destroys a marriage more quickly than dishonesty and infidelity.

St. Augustine teaches that wrongfully concealing the truth and lying are both displeasing to God. *Culpable negligence* occurs when an individual is aware of a serious problem that would cause physical or moral danger to another and does nothing. The delinquent can be legally held responsible for subsequent harm, loss of life or damages.

St. James says it is hypocritical to bless God with a tongue in prayer and then malign people who are created in His image and likeness.[217] How can an individual who is deceitful, stirs up trouble and acts like a spy be trusted?

One Lie often Leads to Many Others

Devils are liars who plot the downfall of individuals by encouraging them to lie. Some people lie so frequently it is hard to detect truth in their words since one lie often breeds another.

In an age of unprecedented surveillance, never go anywhere that is improper nor engage in questionable activities. It is easier to defend a person's actions when the individual has done nothing wrong than to make futile attempts to cover one's tracks or clear one's name when the evidence clearly tells a different story. Character matters. A person's reputation for honesty and integrity edifies others, gives peace of soul and instills trust in others.

Sin Attacks Its Perpetrators

Scientific research has found that liars and dishonest persons live in turmoil and even their bodies are affected by their duplicity. Stress levels increase dramatically for those who live in dread of being uncovered, realize their reputation can be destroyed, their job lost, their marriage broken, their dreams shattered, or that they may be arrested for crimes.

Lying and dishonesty, besides being offensive to God and a cause of civil and domestic discord, attacks its perpetrators. Dishonesty can bring on severe anxiety, high blood pressure and insomnia or cause cancer cells to form.

---

[215] Chapter 19, Verse 11.
[216] Ephesians 4, 25.
[217] James 3, 9-11.

Common Sins Against Charity

Sins of the tongue are very common, especially in today's society. *Rash judgment* analyzes the actions of another and imputes an evil intention. *Detraction* reveals the hidden faults of a person. *Slander*, also called *calumny*, fabricates lies about another. *Gossip* spreads tales or misquotes another in order to defame a person.

Although these sins are common today, each can become mortal if the three conditions—serious offense, knowledge that the offense is serious and full consent are present. Those who have destroyed the reputation of another are required to restore that person's good name.

When the evil life of another is common knowledge, there is no obligation for restitution since the individual destroyed his or her own reputation. Yet, no one should speak of the faults of another except under two conditions: to warn others of danger or to tell those in authority so they can stop abuses and protect those under their care.

Many Americans loathe election years because candidates frequently tell little about their stand and merely broadcast the shortcomings of their opponent. Moral integrity is rare.

Although everyone needs a friend and confidant, others should never be excluded. Favoritism is the enemy of Christian charity. It acts like a toxin, poisoning relationships.

Judging, placing oneself above others and engaging in hollow friendships leads to dissipation. Hatred, jealousy, envy, and criticism of others destroy tranquility and cause unhappiness.

Always be Honest and Truthful

There is nothing comparable to one living as a true follower of Christ, honest in both word and deed. Once sins are confessed and atoned for, one is able to enjoy true, interior peace. A life of integrity brings tranquility and inspires others.

Never Speak Behind Someone's Back

Nothing should be said in the presence of others that wouldn't be said in another's absence. As a bishop attended a dinner he overheard one of the guests berating someone who was absent. The bishop quickly sent a messenger to invite that person to the table. When he arrived the bishop told the guest to repeat the remarks that were said in the other man's absence. In response, he ashamedly left the table. The event made a lasting impression on all.

Chapter Twenty-Two
The Sixth and Ninth Commandments

"Thou shalt not commit adultery." Exodus 20, 14

"Thou shalt not covet thy neighbor's wife." Exodus 20, 17

God created humans male and female and gave them a natural, mutual attraction so that the race could be perpetuated. Due to the Fall of Adam, all humans also have a tendency to lust and to the other Capital Sins. Therefore, they must control their lives and not follow unruly passions. Scripture gives many reminders: "Walk, then, as children of light." (Ephesians 5, 9)

Our Lord said: "Blessed are the clean of heart for they shall see God." (Matthew 5, 8)

St. Peter tells the faithful to "behave yourselves honorably." (1 Peter 2, 10-11) and fight against sinful desires that war against the soul.

St. Paul taught: "For God has not called us unto uncleanness, but unto holiness. ...he who rejects these things rejects not man but God." (1 Thessalonians 4, 3-5, 7-8) "For this is the will of God, your sanctification, that you abstain from immorality. That every one of you shall learn how to possess his vessel in holiness and honor; not in the passion of lust like the Gentiles who do not know God." (1 Corinthians 6, 18).

God's Plan

God ordained, the act that generates life—the marriage act (sexual intercourse) be very pleasurable so couples would be encouraged to engage in it and bring forth children to populate the earth. The marriage act only is to be legitimately enjoyed by married couples. The end of the marriage act is good—to unite husband and wife and bring life into the world.

Jesus compared the marriage bond to His love for the Church and each individual. The marriage act was established for the propagation of children and to allow the married couple to express their mutual love. The *Catechism of the Council of Trent* says:

> The bond between man and wife is one of the closest, and nothing can be more gratifying to both than to know that they are objects of mutual [between each other] and special [above everyone else] affection.[218]

Sins that are Serious By Nature

Since sins against purity are serious by nature, most are mortal. The exception would be when the two conditions—knowing the matter is serious and full consent are lacking. Our Lord said "...I say to you that anyone who so much as looks with lust upon a woman has already committed adultery with her in his heart." (Matthew 5, 28) St Paul says: "...know this and understand that no fornicator, or unclean person... has any inheritance in the kingdom of Christ and God." (Ephesians 5, 5)

Sins Against Purity

Those who engage in premarital sex (*fornication*) do not have rights to this activity since they lack the lifelong commitment necessary to properly raise children. Married partners are not allowed to have sexual intercourse with others who are not their spouse (*adultery*) since they have taken marriage vows to remain faithful to the person they married. The unmarried and married are not allowed to enjoy sexual pleasure by themselves (*masturbation*).

---

[218] p. 431.

It is a mortal sin to attempt or violently force a person into sexual intercourse (*rape*) and for non-married couples to cohabitate before marriage (*live in sin*). Both are based on lust.

Married couples cannot use artificial means to prevent conception including use of spermicides, condoms, birth control pills, or devices. Couples must complete the marriage act and cannot withdraw prematurely (*onanism*). *Sterilization* is only allowed for medical purposes to remove infected organs, never solely as a means of birth control. *Divorce* is a declaration by the state that a married couple is free to marry again. Unless the previous marriage was invalid or a legitimate annulment granted, the individuals who remarry or live with a different partner are "living in sin" and commit the sin of adultery. Christ condemned remarriage after a valid marriage. "...Whoever puts away his wife and marries another, commits adultery against her; and if a wife puts away her husband, and marries another, she commits adultery."[219]

The effects of sexually transmitted diseases (STDs), AIDS, HIV, human papillomavirus, chlamydia, genital herpes, trichomoniasis, gonnorhea, and syphilis can last a lifetime. There is also danger of a spouse and children being infected.

Other sins against purity include: impure thoughts (full or partial consent), playing indecent music, listening to impure jokes or stories, watching bad movies, immoral DVDs, or indecent TV, visiting impure Internet sites, viewing pornography, looking at filthy magazines, reading impure books, wearing suggestive clothing, and homosexual and lesbian lifestyles.

Parents should check the Internet history of the websites used by their children in order to prevent pornography addiction. There are also a number of other sins against purity. Some are unnatural and seriously sinful.

Drug and alcohol abuse can weaken inhibitions and often lead to acts of impurity. Many who die in unrepentant mortal sin became slaves to impurity. They ignored Jesus' sacrifice on the Cross and defiled their bodies by sinful acts and gave scandal to others. Those enslaved to sin often give up the practice of their Catholic Faith.

A Priceless Diamond

Purity is like a priceless diamond, a treasure that must be preserved at all costs. Without it a person cannot enter Heaven. Many saints have renounced a life of sin including St. Augustine, a Doctor of the Church, St. Mary Magdalene, who was at the foot of the Cross and helped evangelize France, and many others.

Modesty is the habit of dressing and acting becomingly. Unmarried people who are pure lead a life of *chastity*. Married couples who preserve marital fidelity practice *continency*.

One of the best ways to preserve purity is to avoid occasions of sin. Other means include praying five decades of the Rosary daily, frequentation of the Sacraments of Penance and the Holy Eucharist, and attendance at Mass every Sunday. It is necessary to keep custody over one's eyes and ears. The eyes are the windows of the soul and not meant to view sinful images, but rather to see God's wondrous creation.

---

[219] Mark 10, 11-12.

Chapter Twenty-Three

Seventh and Tenth Commandments / Laws of the Church

"Thou shalt not steal."   Exodus 20, 15

"Thou shalt not covet thy neighbor's goods."   Exodus 20, 17

God created the world to provide adequate food, shelter and clothing for every individual. Although some have more material goods, others less, life on earth is only temporary. Everything ultimately belongs to God, even though many seldom make the connection. People are only temporary custodians of material goods since these are given to others after death.

St. Thomas Aquinas teaches that having a sufficiency of material goods is necessary in order to perform virtuous actions. It is difficult to keep one's eyes on Heaven when a person doesn't know where to find the next meal. A person should be content with necessities. Superfluities often blind one and impede his or her flight to God. Attachment to material objects acts like an anchor by holding an individual tightly to the earth.

Money is not evil itself, but a necessary medium of exchange. Greed and avarice are evil and ruin millions of lives. Some people never seem to get enough though they have millions of dollars. Material goods cannot completely satisfy.

Although unemployment is rampant, individuals should try to find work. St. Paul said, "...if any man will not work, neither let him eat."[220]

Covetousness leads people to become greedy and selfish thinking only of themselves. Blinded by the glitter of the world, hoarders become enslaved to the very things they think will bring them happiness.

Few realize that no matter how many possessions a person has, the only thing of value brought into eternity are one's merits. It is difficult for a self-centered person to love God and practice charity.

Sins Against Justice

The Seventh Commandment deals with obligations of justice—to pay just debts[221] and respect the property of others. It forbids stealing, robbery, embezzlement, shoplifting, arson, blackmail, keeping stolen property, not returning what was borrowed, piracy, and all other sins against justice. Fraud regarding weights and measures and the quality and quantity of goods is also prohibited.

Justice demands a full day's work for a full day's pay. Sinful actions against justice attack individuals, families, societies, churches, businesses, institutions, and even the poor.

These sins have different degrees of malice and demand restitution. As St. Augustine says, "Give each his due..."[222] and "without restitution, the sin is not forgiven."[223] A legal axiom says: "Goods cry for their legitimate owner." It is therefore necessary to return borrowed items and pay just debts and loans.

---

[220] 2 Thessalonians 3, 10.
[221] Moral theologians often call this a debt of justice.
[222] *On Free Will,* 1, 27.
[223] Epist. LIV. ad Maced.

Many have an insatiable desire to have the newest and greatest and to be the first at the biggest sale. Consider how crowds mob stores at the introduction of a new product, phone, CD, or video game. These items never bring full satisfaction since they need to be repaired, get lost or stolen, or frequently have to be upgraded to prevent them becoming obsolete.

The Tenth Commandment forbids envy and the desire to have what others possess. Avarice, jealousy and many other sins stem from dissatisfaction with the gifts God has freely given.

The Eye of the Needle

Our Lord said it is easier for a camel to pass through the eye of a needle than for a rich person to enter Heaven. How is this possible?

Jerusalem once had an entrance gate called the *eye of the needle* that was so small that only children and animals could enter the city through it. It was impossible for a camel laden with goods to pass through. It had to be completely unloaded and then the camel had to crawl to enter. This gate typifies detachment of the heart from material possessions.

Antidotes

The antidote for greed is charity. St. Cyprian, St. John Chrysostom, St. Gregory, and others extol the virtue of giving alms. Material goods will never make one happy since humans were created for something infinitely higher—God and eternal life.

God sometimes sends natural disasters to forcibly detach hearts from possessions. He feels it is better for people to lose some "things" here than lose their soul for all eternity.

At the end of time, the earth will be destroyed by fire and nothing will remain but ashes. All the things that once seemed so important, for whose sake lives were sacrificed and souls were lost will be no more.

I Have to Buy More Stock

Once a priest visited a dying non-Catholic who passed away a few days later. The man was so blinded spiritually that instead of preparing for imminent death, he merely kept repeating, "I got to buy more stock… I got to buy more stock." He died a day or two later.

No one really cares who is the wealthiest person in a cemetery. People can't take their wealth with them, only their deeds.

The Laws of the Church

1. To assist at Mass on all Sundays and holydays of obligation

2. To fast and abstain on the days appointed

3. To confess our sins at least once a year

4. To receive Holy Communion during the Easter time

5. To contribute to the support of the Church

6. To observe the laws of the Church concerning marriage

Chapter Twenty-Four
What Causes a Sin to Become Mortal?

For a sin to be mortal, the offense *has to be serious, known to be serious* and a person *must give full consent.* If any of these three elements are lacking, the sin is considered venial. A person cannot commit a sin by accident or while asleep.

Those raised in an atmosphere where sin is commonplace may be unaware of its seriousness. In spite of this, these individuals have an obligation to form their conscience properly. Christ spoke of individuals who lack knowledge of the seriousness of sin when He said from the Cross, "Father, forgive them, for they do not know not what they are doing." (Luke 23, 34)

Moral theologians use the terms *deliberate* and *voluntary* to explain that sin must be a free act emerging from the will. The word *deliberate* is taken from two Latin words that mean "from freedom." The word *voluntary* is derived from the Latin word for "will."

Grave matter entails something that offends God so seriously that it will send the person to Hell if he or she doesn't repent before death. Some sins are obviously serious. Others are not. Basic principles need to be applied in order to determine the gravity of a thought, word, act, or omission. If doubt remains, speak to the priest in the confessional.

Sins of thought can become serious when full consent is given since Our Lord spoke of murders, adulteries, and other sins committed from the heart.[224] A person must resist at once in order to avoid sin since it is hard to control the will once something enticing is presented to it.

Grave Matter

The guideline below, based on principles, deals with grave (serious) matter. Knowledge of the seriousness of the sin and full consent are also necessary for a sin to become mortal.

Most mortal sins offend against the virtues of charity, purity and justice. Others offend God by being contrary to the Ten Commandments or the Laws of the Church in a serious way. Gravity of matter is determined by what a commandment or Law of the Church commands or forbids.

1 Since blasphemy is a voluntary attack against God, it is nearly always a serious sin. Profanation of the Blessed Sacrament and sacrilegious defamation of crucifixes and statues are mortal sins. Use of fortune-tellers, Ouija Boards or tarot cards manifests a lack of trust in God and if known to be seriously sinful become so.

Catholics who worship in non-Catholic churches demonstrate apathy toward God. Since Jesus founded the Catholic Church He expects His followers to worship there and believe His teachings. It is also a danger to the faith for Catholics to take part in non-Catholic bible study. Protestant scriptures are incomplete[225] and they have completely different concepts regarding faith, grace, justification, the Blessed Trinity, Mass, sacraments, a visible church, sin, and many other elements of Catholicism.

2 It is grave matter to habitually use the name of God in vain and make no effort to stop.

3 It is a serious act of ingratitude to God to purposely miss Mass on Sundays and Holy Days.

---

[224] Our Lord said: "For out of the heart come evil thoughts, murders, adulteries, immorality, thefts, false witness, blasphemies." (Matthew 15, 19) "But I say to you that anyone who looks with lust at a woman has already committed adultery with her in his heart." (Matthew 5, 28).

[225] Protestant Bibles are missing the books of Baruch, Ecclesiasticus, Judith, First and Second Machabees, Tobias, Wisdom, and parts of Daniel and Esther.

Working on Sunday unnecessarily can become a serious sin if it is prolonged for more than two hours or grave scandal is caused.

4   It can become grave matter if an older child strikes a parent. They deserve love and respect for bringing children into the world and for the care they give. If full reflection were absent the sin would be venial. It is a serious sin of neglect if parents don't provide for their children and may be a serious sin of neglect if children don't provide for their parents when it is necessary and when they are able to do so.

5   Grave matter against charity would be to ruin or seriously attempt to tarnish the reputation of another, do serious bodily harm, or willingly cause the death of another. Abortion takes a human life and is grave matter. Sadly, many think they have a right to kill unwanted children. This shows how far people have drifted from God. It is grave matter to unnecessarily risk one's life or that of another, or to take it by murder or suicide. Abusing drugs, drinking to excess and driving under the influence of drugs or alcohol are serious matter because of the harm they may cause to oneself and others.

6/9   Sins against purity are serious by their very nature. Viewing pornography, committing masturbation, premarital sex, adultery, the use of artificial birth control, sodomy, withdrawal, homosexual or lesbian acts, doing anything that frustrates the proper use of the marital act, and other sexual sins are serious offenses against God. Sexual pleasure is only to be enjoyed by validly married couples.

7/10   Serious matter against the seventh commandment includes stealing, vandalism or, purposely damaging the goods or property of another out of envy or jealousy unless the dollar amount was very small. Grave matter against justice includes unjust usury, neglecting to pay one's just debts when able and stealing when the amount is sizeable. Stealing a number of inexpensive things over a period of time will become mortal once the value of the stolen items becomes sizeable.

8   Lying under oath—perjury is grave matter since one takes God as witness for something known to be false.

It is grave matter to purposely eat meat on Friday unless it is a Holy Day or one that is customarily dispensed.

It is a sin of sacrilege to make a bad confession by purposely omitting to confess a mortal sin. The omission of the Easter Duty—annual confession of sins and reception of Holy Communion during the Eastertime, is grave matter. Knowingly receiving Holy Communion in the state of mortal sin is a very serious sin of sacrilege. It is a profanation of God's greatest gift of love.

Neglect of the obligation of supporting the church can become serious if it is habitual. If indigent, one can support the church through volunteer work.

A Devil Teaches a Lesson

A devil once spoke through a possessed person lamenting that separation from God was even worse than the terrible fires of Hell. The demon stated that he would gladly suffer for over 10,000 years just to see God for a moment. "If I had a body like you I would always be at His feet begging for mercy. Oh, if men only knew what it is to lose the grace of God!"[226]

---

226 Very Rev. Charles Callan, OP, *Illustrations for Sermons and Instructions*, p. 97.

Chapter Twenty-Five

Spiritual Blindness

Spiritual blindness is very real and common today. Millions walk in darkness and seem content to do so. Few today love God or include Him in their daily lives. Most are preoccupied with themselves and die unprepared. Where will they spend eternity?

One should rather watch and pray to prepare for the Lord's coming at Judgment by leading a virtuous life and earning merit in order to glorify God and be eternally rewarded in Heaven.

Sin's Powerful Pull

By sinning, a person chooses sin and self over God. Vice, based on pride and self-gratification, places one's own will above God's. A precipitous downward plunge often follows as one becomes hardened by repeated rejection of grace.

Sin becomes almost second nature when a person, preoccupied with self, attempts to stifle conscience and habitually goes against the law of God. Enveloped in an empty existence, the person eventually drifts away from God, family and friends.

God still pursues the sinner and calls, but the individual's line is usually "busy" with no time for God or the supernatural. Unless a person turns to prayer, it is very easy to lose one's immortal soul in this state.

Spiritually Blind and Deaf

A person needs to accept God's invitation to return, but most turn a deaf ear and remain immersed in sin. "They have eyes and see not. They have ears and hear not."[227]

Many use noise, distractions and loud music, or drug or alcohol abuse to mute the voice of God and conscience. Endless pursuit of pleasure gives people little time to focus on what is really important—the salvation of their immortal soul. It is similar to a person getting into a car and driving aimlessly with no destination in mind.

Sinful Pleasure

Sin's greatest allurement, sinful pleasure, often leads to loss of self-control and addiction. Many become so spiritually blinded, they accept being condemned to the eternal fires of Hell and forfeiting the joys of Heaven in order to enjoy the temporary pleasure of mortal sin.

Sinful pleasure is a poison that destroys one from within. Those immersed in it never find happiness since sins breed punishment, remorse and sadness.

God wants people to be happy and offers legitimate channels. Only He can fill one with interior joy and peace of soul.

Walking in Darkness

Spiritual blindness darkens the understanding, weakens the will and often causes those infected to become slaves to impurity.[228] Those who consistently reject God and His laws walk in darkness with no guide and no light.

---

[227] Psalm 113.
[228] See Ephesians 4, 18-19.

In the state of sin danger looms everywhere. Sounds that used to be pleasing become ominous. Activities that used to be enjoyable become causes of dread apprehension. In spite of attempts to silence conscience, there are still frequent reminders. Although God's judgment is looming, the person is often too callous to care.

Spiritual blindness is a vicious circle that fosters depression, immorality, and alcohol and drug abuse. It leads to separation from God and can cause one to be confined to eternal Hellfire.

The book of Wisdom laments the fate of the damned. "What hath pride profited us? or what advantage hath the boasting of riches brought us? All those things are passed away like a shadow. ...[229]."

Return to God

One must continue to pray for loved ones, friends and others who have drifted from God, for as long as life remains there is hope. Once a person who has fallen has returned to God, the Rosary, Sunday Mass and the Sacraments of Penance and Holy Eucharist will restore to that individual the grace, peace of soul and happiness that were previously lacking. The vacuum caused by sin and worldliness will be replaced with God's love and forgiveness. An empty, meaningless life will again become enriched and worthwhile.

St. Paul encourages his followers to "...be renewed in the spirit of your mind. Put on the new man, which has been created according to God in justice and holiness of truth."[230] Although everyone is weak and has a tendency to evil due to original sin, God reminded St. Paul: "My grace is sufficient for thee, for strength is made perfect in weakness."[231] Prayer gives needed heavenly strength to help one practice virtue and observe the Ten Commandments.

Sight is one of the most precious gifts bestowed by God. Through it a person can view the wonders God created and move about safely and confidently. Spiritual sight helps a person put life into perspective. It encourages one to avoid evil and persevere in doing good. It keeps one's eyes on the goal—reaching the eternal happiness of Heaven.

Unique Wake Up Call

Scripture records the tales of countless monarchs and kings who fought against God and lost. One such individual was Nebuchadnezzar, the Babylonian monarch who foolishly claimed to be a god and commanded his subjects to worship him.

God punished the king's pride by turning him into an animal for a period of time as recorded in the book of Daniel.[232] He grew feathers and claws, was obliged to eat grass and had to walk on all fours. Eventually his spiritual blindness was cured, he acknowledged the true God and was restored to his former state. Others are not so fortunate.

---

[229] Chapter 5, Verses 8-9.
[230] Ephesians 4, 23-24
[231] 2 Corinthians 12, 9.
[232] Chapter 4, Verses 29-34.

Chapter Twenty-Six

Saints

Saints are the men, women and children who lived holy lives on earth, died in the state of sanctifying grace and now enjoy the beatific vision of God in Heaven. Due to their close relationship with God, saints have great intercessory power.

They glorify God in the same way as parents are honored through the accomplishments of their children. God honors the saints in numerous ways. He is pleased when others pray to them or revere their memory.

God honors the saints by performing countless miracles through their intercession. Respect shown them reflects back to Him. He is pleased that people invoke their intercession. God has even allowed the bodies of 72 saints to remain incorrupt (their bodies have not decayed) including St. Francis Xavier and St. Bernadette.[233]

The Use of Statues and Sacred Images

The Catholic Church honors the saints and wants individuals to draw inspiration from their virtuous lives. Depictions of saints are placed in churches and homes to remind the faithful of their goodness so they can imitate their virtuous lives and confidently invoke their powerful intercession. St. Gregory said statues in Catholic churches help laity better learn their faith.

Fr. Birkhauser gives a further explanation.

> The use of images in the Church dates from very remote antiquity. This is sufficiently proved from the monuments of the Apostolic Age, and from the numerous symbols and images of Christ, the [Blessed] Virgin, the Apostles and biblical personages which adorn the Roman Catacombs; many of these symbols belong to the first and second centuries.[234]

These images include Noah and the Ark, Daniel in the Lion's Den, the Nativity of Jesus, the Three Kings, and frescos of the Good Shepherd, Mary, and St. Joseph.

The Second Council of Nicaea in 787 AD declared that the cross, statues and images should be placed in churches, on vestments, in homes, and along roads. It is inspiring to see statues and holy images adorning the grounds of Catholic cemeteries instead of simple gravestones.

Contemporary Use of Statues

Statuary and monuments are used by current society to honor heroes, heroines, world leaders, athletes, and other famous persons. They are found in city squares, sports' halls of fame, museums, cemeteries, stadiums, lawns, schools, and even airports, and hospitals. No one worships these depictions. They are merely ways to remember individuals who have had an impact on history and society. Statues and images of Christ, Mary and the saints should be regarded in a similar manner.

Photographs are used to remember loved ones and friends, and are respectfully carried in lockets, wallets and purses worldwide. Holy cards are used in a similar manner to remember and attempt to imitate the virtues of saintly men and women.

---

[233] For further reference see Joan Cruz' book *The Incorruptibles*.
[234] *History of the Church*, p. 313.

Iconoclasts

Heretics often promoted the false idea that Our Lady and saints diminish God's honor and are His rivals. Thousands of statues and relics were destroyed by eighth century iconoclasts and in the sixteenth century by Protestants during the Reformation.

Stone statues on the outer walls of cathedrals in France were often used for target practice during the French Revolution. Communist soldiers in Spain fired at the Sacred Heart statue in Madrid in the late 1930s to exhibit their hatred for Our Lord.

Modernists revived iconoclasm after Vatican II by removing statues and crucifixes. Many modern churches now resemble dance halls or airplane hangars.

God has Given Special Roles to Certain Saints

A *patron saint* is one a Catholic is named after or one to whom a person has a special devotion. Some examples of help given by saints include:

St. Joseph assists those in need.	St. Anne watches over mariners.
St. Jude helps with hopeless cases.	St. Anthony finds lost items.
St. Therese of Lisieux leads souls to Jesus.	St. Francis de Sales teaches patience.
St. Maria Goretti helps her clients preserve purity.	St. Lucy aids those with eye ailments.
St. Zita guides mothers and housewives.	St. Gerard assists expectant mothers.

The Human Body is Sacred

Saints honored God on earth by their virtuous and edifying lives. In return they will receive a glorified body in heaven after the Last Judgment. Their bodies are therefore sacred since they were the abode of their immortal souls. The Council of Trent declared:

> The bodies of the holy martyrs and others now living with Christ [saints] which bodies were the living members of Christ and temples of the Holy Ghost and which are by Him to be raised to eternal life and to be glorified, are to be venerated by the faithful; for through these bodies many benefits are bestowed by God on men...[235]

Catholics are buried after death. The body is not just a wrapper that is disposed of or incinerated. Even though cremation is very common today, it shows disrespect for the deceased and leaves nearly no remembrance of the departed.

Relics

Museums house memorabilia of important personages thereby preserving history for future generations. The pen that was used for the signing of the Declaration of Independence and the Liberty Bell in Philadelphia are two such relics.

Relics of the saints are divided into three classes. The remains of the body of a saint are called *first class relics*. These are often encased behind glass and adorned with silk. The Catholic Church verifies the authenticity of first class relics with papers that are written in Latin and contain the seal of a cardinal or other prelate.

A *second class relic* is an article of clothing or something else used by a saint. A *third class relic* is something that touched a *first* or *second class* relic.

---

[235] Session 25.

The history of the Church relates countless miracles performed by saints, by invoking their intercession or by use of their relics. *The Catechism of the Council of Trent* relates miracles performed at the tombs of the martyrs where many were healed, the dead brought back to life and demons expelled. Saints Augustine and Ambrose witnessed some of these.[236]

St. Januarius, bishop of Naples, who was martyred for his faith in 305 AD, annually performs a miracle on his feast day of September 19. The sand-like dried blood liquefies once the archbishop of Naples places an ampule of the saint's dried blood next to his other relics on the main altar. This miracle was first reported in 1389 and occurs annually unless an impending calamity takes place. Although St. Januarius was "decanonized" by the Modern Church, there was such an uproar that the Vatican allowed the residents of Naples to continue to revere him.

The Communion of Saints

The term *Communion of Saints* is often misunderstood. It is the union of the saints in Heaven (*Church Triumphant*), faithful Catholics on Earth (*Church Militant*) and the Souls in Purgatory (*Church Suffering*).

There are nearly 2,000 saints found in the *Roman Martyrology,* the official register of saints. From 1588-1958, popes canonized 296 saints and beatified 808 (the step before canonization).

The process of canonization has three steps: *venerable, blessed* and *saint* and can take decades or even centuries to complete. Four verifiable miracles are needed for canonization. A person called the "devil's advocate" used to carefully scrutinize the lives of the candidates for sainthood. The Modern Church completely revamped the entire canonization process after Vatican II. As a result, more saints were canonized during the reign of John Paul II than during the preceding four hundred years.

Various Categories of Saints Found in Prayer Books

Saints are listed in various precise Roman classifications.

Abbot	one who governed a monastery
Bishop	successor of the Apostles
Virgin	woman who vowed her virginity to God
Doctor[237]	a teacher of the Catholic Faith
Martyr[238]	one who gave his or her life for the faith
Confessor	a priest or male lay person who professed the Catholic Faith
Holy Women	saintly females who were neither virgins nor martyrs
Supreme Pontiff[239]	pope

St. Jerome summarizes Catholic teaching regarding the saints:

> We do not worship, we do not adore, we do not bow down before the creature rather than to the Creator, but we venerate the relics of the martyrs in order better to adore Him whose martyrs they are.[240]

---

[236] Fr. Clement Raab, OFM, *Twenty General Councils of the Catholic Church,* pp. 57-58.
[237] Doctor is derived from the Latin word for *teacher.*
[238] Martyr is derived from the Greek word for *witness.*
[239] Pontiff is derived from two Latin words that mean *bridge builder.*
[240] *Ad Riparium,* IX.

Worship Shown to God / Honor Given to Saints

There are three classifications Catholics should understand regarding God and the Saints.

Latria   *worship* offered to God alone. Catholics worship the Blessed Trinity and show honor to God by means of genuflecting, kneeling and the use of incense in church.

Hyperdulia   *honor* shown to Mary reflects back to Jesus, her Son. Our Lady ranks above all other saints.

Dulia   *honor* shown to saints by individuals who seek their intercession by prayer.

Mary's Role

Every word of Holy Scripture has important meaning. St. Matthew describes the entrance of the Magi, the Three Wise Men, who came to worship the newborn Messias.[241]

> And entering the house, they found the Child with Mary His mother, and falling down they worshipped Him. And opening their treasures they offered Him, gold, frankincense and myrrh.

Pope Pius X encouraged all to follow the example of the Magi when he wrote, "...it only remains for us to receive Christ from the hands of Mary."[242]

St. Germanus said that since humans are unworthy, they need a mediator with Christ. Who could better fulfill that role than His sinless mother? Mary, who is so close to the throne of God, has tremendous power to assist those who invoke her intercession.

Jesus Christ is the Redeemer, the one Mediator with God the Father.[243] In order to honor His Mother who dedicated her entire life to Him and suffered with Him, Our Lord chose to have Mary dispense the merits He earned during His Passion and life on earth.

Numerous popes and St. Alphonsus Ligouri, St. Bernard and St. Robert Bellarmine address Mary as Mediatrix of All Graces, the channel through whom the graces of God are distributed.

In everyday life it is often necessary to have someone with "connections" make an introduction or arrange a meeting with an important personage. A person can "go to the top," but will usually be rejected. Knowing someone who has an "in" often opens the door. Saints act like God's ambassadors. God is honored when we ask their intercession.

Catholics do not worship Mary or the saints, but ask them to intercede with God and assist us. They do not detour from God, but provide paths that lead individuals closer to Him.

To Jesus Through Mary

Although some claim, Catholics give Mary too much honor, the result of true devotion to Mary is a greater love for Jesus. Rosary processions end in church and the Blessing of the Sick following the Rosary is performed using a monstrance that houses the Blessed Sacrament.

Those who pray the daily Rosary usually faithfully receive the Sacraments of Penance and the Holy Eucharist and love to spend time in church in front of the tabernacle. Catholics don't worship Mary. They respectfully honor her so she can better lead them to her Son.

---

[241] Chapter 2, Verse 11.
[242] *Ad Diem illum.*
[243] 1 Timothy 2, 5.

Chapter Twenty-Seven

The Seven Sacraments

Our Lord instituted Seven Sacraments in order to offer special graces that assist souls to merit Heaven. Each sacrament has a specific role to help a Catholic from birth to death.

Baptism washes away original sin from the soul and makes one an adopted child of God. *Penance* forgives the sins committed after Baptism by the absolution of the priest. The *Holy Eucharist* contains the Body, Blood, Soul, and Divinity of Jesus Christ under the appearance of bread and wine. *Confirmation* strengthens the faith of its recipient. *Matrimony* blesses the lifelong marriage contract and ensures the propagation of the human race. *Holy Orders* provides ministers to offer Mass and dispense the sacraments. *Extreme Unction* prepares one to enter eternity.

Essential Elements of Each Sacrament

Every sacrament is composed of specific elements that are necessary for validity—*matter, form, intention,* and *minister.* These vary with each sacrament. If there is an essential change to any of these, the sacrament is invalid.

Matter for Each Sacrament

Baptism	water (preferably baptismal water)
Penance	repentant sin
Holy Eucharist	unleavened bread and natural grape wine
Confirmation	Holy Chrism (mixture of olive oil and balsam)
Matrimony	lifelong marital contract
Holy Orders	imposition of hands by the bishop
Extreme Unction	Oil of the Sick

Form for Each Sacrament

Baptism	*Name* I baptize thee in the name of the Father and of the Son and of the Holy Ghost.[244]
Penance	Words of Absolution
Holy Eucharist	Words of Consecration
Confirmation	I sign thee with the sign of the Cross and I confirm thee with the chrism of salvation in the name of the Father and of the Son and of the Holy Ghost.[245]
Matrimony	Marriage Vows
Holy Orders	Words of the Special Preface recited by the bishop
Extreme Unction	Words used at the anointings

---

[244] *N. Ego te baptizo in nomine Patris, et Filii, et Spiritus Sancti.*
[245] *N. Signo te signo cru+cis et confirmo te Chrismate salutis. In nomine Pa+tris, et Fi+lii, et Spiritus+Sancti.*

Intention for Each Sacrament

A minister must have the intention to do what the Church does or what Christ intends. If a person makes a contrary or indeterminate intention, the sacrament is invalid since it no longer becomes what Christ intended.

Minister for Each Sacrament

The priest is the normal minister for Baptism, Penance, Holy Eucharist, Matrimony, and Extreme Unction.[246] The bishop is the minister of Confirmation and Holy Orders. The married couple confer the Sacrament of Matrimony on each other. In danger of death, anyone can confer Baptism as long as the person follows the rite exactly and has the intention to do what Christ intends.[247]

The worthiness of the minister has no effect on the validity of a sacrament as long as the person has been validly consecrated a bishop or validly ordained a priest.[248]

Sacraments Confer Grace

Theologians use the Latin terms *ex opere operato*[249] to indicate, sacraments that are validly confected, give sanctifying grace and sacramental grace (that corresponds to each sacrament). If one is unrepentant or knowingly receives the Holy Eucharist, Confirmation, Matrimony, Holy Orders, or Extreme Unction in the state of mortal sin, the recipient receives no grace from these sacraments until he or she has made a good confession.

The Dispositions of the Recipient are Important

The dispositions of the recipient can increase the amount of grace received from a sacrament. This is called *ex opere operantis*.[250] St. Cyril of Jerusalem encourages recipients to prepare properly for each sacrament and fervently receive them in order to earn abundant graces.

Three Oils Used in the Sacraments

OS	**Oleum Sanctum**	*Oil of Catechumens* or *Holy Oil* is used at Baptism and Holy Orders.
SC	**Sanctum Chrisma**	*Holy Chrism* is used at Baptism, Confirmation and the Consecration of a Bishop.
OI	**Oleum Infirmorum**	*Oil of the Sick* is used in Extreme Unction.

Sacraments are precise and exact because Christ made them that way. They are not mere expressions of faith. They give God's grace.

---

[246] On September 14, 1946, the Congregation of the Sacraments gave priests permission to confirm those in danger of death when no bishop is available.

[247] If there is doubt if a person is alive the priest says: *Si vivis, ego te baptizo in nomine Pa+tris, et Fi+lii, et Spiritus+Sancti.*

[248] The Donatist heresy, started by Bishop Donatus, erroneously claimed that sinful ministers rendered a sacrament invalid. The Catholic Church teaches that an unworthy minister commits a sacrilege by administering a sacrament while in the state of mortal sin, but the sacrament is still validly conferred.

[249] *Through the rite having been accomplished.*

[250] *From the efforts of the person.*

Chapter Twenty-Eight

Baptism

Our Lord stressed the importance of Baptism before ascending into Heaven when He told the Apostles to "Go therefore, and make disciples of all nations, baptizing them in the name of the Father, and of the Son, and of the Holy Spirit, teaching them to observe all that I have commanded you..."[251] St. Paul spoke of "...one Lord, one faith, one Baptism."[252]

The word *baptism* is derived from the Greek word *to wash*. Jesus determined the intention, decided on the use of water and chose specific words to be used at the ceremony.

Infant Baptism dates back to *Apostolic Times*. Catholic parents have a serious obligation to have their children baptized within two weeks of a child's birth because Baptism is necessary for salvation. Jesus Christ said, "Amen, amen I say to thee, unless a man be born again of water and the Spirit, he cannot enter into the kingdom of God."[253]

The sacrament should not be postponed until children are older. Adults and older children who wish to be baptized must receive adequate instruction. They must also desire to be baptized and be sorry for all their sins since Baptism forgives the sins of the person who receives it.

Effects of Baptism

1) Takes away original sin, all personal sin and punishment due to sin

2) Infuses sanctifying grace and faith, hope and charity into the soul

3) Makes the recipient an adopted child of God and an heir of Heaven

4) One becomes a temple of the Holy Ghost and holy and pleasing to God

5) Imprints a permanent mark on the soul

Our Lord established Baptism to remove original sin from the soul—the sin inherited from Adam that makes one an enemy of God. Baptism also gives sanctifying grace, making the baptized person part of God's royal family. This is symbolized by the royal wedding garment mentioned by St. Matthew[254] that is necessary for admission into Heaven.

Three Manners of Conferring Baptism

Infusion The form commonly used today. The priest pours water over the forehead of the recipient while simultaneously pronouncing the form. Water must flow over the skin of the forehead for the sacrament to be valid.

Immersion An individual walks into a body of water while the bishop, priest or deacon pronounces the form. This practice was frequently used in the early Church. Widespread use ended in the thirteenth century.

Aspersion The practice of sprinkling baptismal water over the forehead while pronouncing the baptismal formula is discouraged since there is danger that the water may not properly flow over the skin of the recipient.

---

[251] Matthew 28, 19-20.
[252] Ephesians 4, 15.
[253] John 3, 5.
[254] Chapter 22, 1-14.

Types of Baptism

Solemn   Conferred by a bishop or priest. The deacon is considered the extraordinary minister of Baptism.

Emergency   Anyone can baptize when there is imminent danger of death. There has to be
(Private)   an assurance of the Catholic upbringing of the individual in the event the person survives. The parents have a serious obligation to have a priest perform the additional ceremonies as soon as possible.[255]

Conditional   When a reasonable doubt remains whether a previous Baptism was valid or not, a *Conditional Baptism* is performed. The normal ceremonies of Baptism are observed, but when it comes to the actual baptismal ceremony, different words are used. *(Name)* If you are not baptized, I baptize you in the name of the Father and of the Son and of the Holy Ghost.[256]

If the previous Baptism was invalid, the conditional one validly baptizes the individual. If the previous Baptism was valid, nothing occurs.

Special Ceremonies Used during the Baptism of Infants

It is customary in the United States for infants, children and adults to be baptized using the ceremony for the Baptism of Infants. The Baptism of Adults ceremonies are quite lengthy.

During the Baptism, the priest wears a white surplice and a reversible violet and white stole. The violet side is worn during the opening ceremonies and the white side is used from the short Profession of Faith until the rite is completed.

Although the *Priest's New Ritual* and the *Collectio Rituum* give an English translation of part of the ceremony, the exorcisms, anointings and essential form of the rite must be recited in Latin. The ritual gives the plural form for some prayers if more than one person is being baptized. Other prayers are in singular form and must be said over each individual.

Baptismal Sponsors   Every person being baptized in the Catholic Church must have two sponsors—one male and one female. These are often called Godparents. Parents and spouses cannot act as sponsors.

Sponsors are baptized Catholics who have attained the use of reason[257] and will ensure the Catholic upbringing of the person being baptized in the event, the parents die or stop practicing the faith. They should be exemplary, practicing Catholics.

The Godmother holds the baby during the ceremonies to symbolize spiritual relationship. The Godfather is to touch the shoulder of the person being baptized while the water is being poured.

Sponsors reply to the questions of the priest unless the individual is able to respond. If a sponsor cannot attend the ceremony for a good reason, another may act as proxy.

---

[255] Canon 759.
[256] *N. Si non est baptizatus* (for a male, *baptizata* for a female) *ego te baptizo in nomine Patris, et Filii, et Spiritus Sancti.*
[257] Canon Law says a sponsor should be at least 14 years of age unless there is a good reason for an exception.

The *Catechism of the Council of Trent* reminds sponsors of their serious obligation before God. Due to loss of faith or negligence of parents, godparents may need to be actively involved in the spiritual welfare of their godchildren. This may include instruction, encouragement or advice.

Ceremonies Begin   in the church vestibule to symbolize that the unbaptized person is not yet a member of the Catholic Church.

Questions   The person who wants to be baptized is asked: What is your name?
                              What do you ask of the Church of God?   Faith.
                              What does faith offer you?   Life everlasting.

Sufflation   The priest blows over the person three times in the form of cross praying that the devil departs and the Holy Ghost enters the soul.

Signs of the Cross   The priest makes numerous signs of the Cross on the forehead of the person being baptized to remind him that Jesus redeemed mankind.

Imposition of the Hand   of the priest symbolizes his authority.

Blessed Salt   is placed on the tongue of the person being baptized to symbolize the necessity of preserving sanctifying grace.

Exorcisms   There are several exorcisms during the ceremony. These are commands by the priest that the devil leave the individual.

Entrance into church   Sponsors hold the end of the priest's stole and proceed to the baptismal font praying the Apostles Creed and Our Father.

Ephpheta   The priest touches the ears and nostrils of the person being baptized in imitation of the like actions of Christ. This symbolizes opening one's ears to the grace of God.

Anointing with Holy Oil   The priest anoints the person to be baptized with Holy Oil (OS) on the lower neck and on the back of the neck between the shoulder's. This symbolizes that each Catholic is precious in the sight of God.

Renunciation of the Devil The person to be baptized makes a formal renunciation of the devil, of his temptations and display (pomps) and works. Baptismal vows are annually renewed during the Easter Vigil.

Profession of Faith   The priest changes to the white stole and asks the individual who will soon be baptized if he or she believes in the Blessed Trinity: Father, Son and Holy Ghost. The person is then asked if he or she wants to be baptized.

The Baptism   The priest or person performing the Baptism says the Christian name of the person being baptized and continues reciting the form while simultaneously pouring baptismal water over the skin on the person's forehead three times in the form of a cross.

The Name of a Saint   is given to the child by its parents since the Church wants each Catholic to have a heavenly patron to be inspired by the holy life of the individual. The middle name of the person being baptized only needs to be said by the priest during the first inquiry (at the beginning of the rite), during the actual baptism and at the dismissal.

The Godmother should tilt the head of the child over the baptismal font so the water can flow easily over the skin. The priest afterwards wipes the individual's forehead with a towel.

Anointing with Holy Chrism	Following the Baptism, the priest recites a prayer and anoints the crown of the head of the newly baptized person with Holy Chrism in the form of a cross.
White Garment	A white linen cloth is placed on the head of the baptized individual to symbolize baptismal innocence (remaining in the state of grace, free from mortal sin).
Lighted Candle	A lighted decorative candle is presented to the Godparents (during the Baptism of Infants) or to the individual who has been baptized (if they have attained the use of reason). It symbolizes, Christ is the Light of the World and that the newly baptized person should be a good example by leading a life of virtue. The family keeps the baptismal candle once the ceremony concludes.

Reception of Converts

The Catholic Church has special laws and procedures for the reception of converts. Since some Protestant baptisms are valid, a priest must investigate each.

1) If the convert has never been baptized or the previous Baptism has been found to be invalid, the person receives the Catholic rite of Baptism.

2) If the previous Baptism remains doubtful, the convert makes an Abjuration of Error or Profession of Faith, receives conditional absolution from censures, is conditionally baptized, and receives the Sacrament of Penance with conditional absolution.

3) If the previous Baptism was valid, the convert makes an Abjuration of Error or Profession of Faith, is absolved from censures, receives the Sacrament of Penance with absolution, and then the ceremonies of Baptism are supplied.[258]

---

[258] The priest goes through the rite of Baptism (anointings, prayers, etc.) with the convert but omits the baptismal ceremony.

Chapter Twenty-Nine
Penance
God Expects a Virtuous Life

God expects humans to ask for His grace in prayer, obey the Ten Commandments and follow His designs. The Book of Genesis says: "I am the Almighty God: walk before Me, and be perfect."[259] During the Sermon on the Mount, Jesus repeated this message. "You therefore are to be perfect, even as your Heavenly Father is perfect."[260] The Fourth Lateran Council interprets this quote to mean: "Be perfect by the perfection of grace as your Heavenly Father is perfect by the perfection of nature."[261]

Nothing defiled shall enter Heaven. Atonement must be made for sin in this life or the next. God does not desire the eternal death of sinners, but wants them to be converted and live.[262] Holy Scripture tells us to seek God while He may be found, and call upon Him in prayer while He is near. Everyone has free will, but after death it is too late to repent.

Sacrament of Mercy and Forgiveness

The Sacrament of Penance[263] forgives sin and also gives special graces to help one avoid sin in the future. It gives an individual the chance to repent and return to God. One's salvation may depend on using this sacrament efficaciously.

Penance is the sacrament whereby sins, committed after Baptism, are forgiven by God through the absolution of the priest. The *Catechism of the Council of Trent* compares this sacrament to a plank after a shipwreck. Since so many lose their baptismal innocence by mortal sin, Penance is the only means of being assured of regaining God's friendship.

Our Lord frequently forgave sins when He lived on earth and He gave that same power to Catholic priests and bishops. On Easter, Christ said to the Apostles and their successors: "Receive the Holy Spirit; whose sins you shall forgive, they are forgiven them and whose sins you shall retain, they are retained."[264] Jesus gave St. Peter the Keys of the Kingdom of Heaven,[265] therefore, priests and bishops share the *power of the keys* by having the commission and authority to forgive sin.[266]

Confession reopens the Gates of Heaven to one who has committed mortal sin, repented and received absolution. The many special graces bestowed by the Sacrament of Penance also helps protect a person from falling into Hell.

Catholics must go to confession at least once a year. This is a serious obligation binding under pain of sin. Confession done over the phone is invalid.

Sin

It is necessary to understand the great evil and malice of sin since many people today justify it as just being part of everyday life. Sin is open rebellion against God; it is defiance of His laws. God is infinite, so every sin is, in a sense, an infinite offense.

---

259 Chapter 17, Verse 1.
260 Matthew 5, 48.
261 *Conc. Lateran. IV, cap. Damnamus,* (Denzinger-Bannwart, *Enchiridion,* n. 432.)
262 Ezechiel 33, 11.
263 Commonly known as confession.
264 John 20, 23.
265 Matthew 16, 19.
266 See Matthew 18, 18. See Canon George Smith, DD, PhD, *The Teaching of the Catholic Church: Volume II,* pp. 957-958.

Since God is offended by every sin, there is a penalty attached to each. Venial sins will be atoned for in the temporary fire of Purgatory. Unrepentant mortal sins will be punished in the eternal fires of Hell. It is not something to be taken lightly.

Sin is not neutral since it can destroy an individual and harm one's family, friends, community, and job. Repeated sinful actions form bad habits that can lead to addiction.

People can become apathetic to the dangers of sin, its evil nature and deadly consequences especially since society downplays its gravity today. Many become slaves to sin.

Sin must be overcome by self-control. This is achieved by means of prayer, avoidance of occasions of sin, frequentation of the Sacraments of Penance and Holy Eucharist, and constant vigilance. A good life gives peace of soul. An evil life creates regret and remorse.

The Confessional Seal

It is important to realize the priest has the power to forgive all sins and they remain under the *confessional seal*. Every sin that has been confessed remains confidential and will never be told to anyone. St. John Nepomucene of Bohemia died defending the confessional seal.

Satisfaction

Satisfaction is derived from two Latin words that mean *doing enough*. God is all-just and He demands restitution for sins committed against justice including embezzlement, stealing, vandalism, etc. The sinner must repay the person or company harmed, or if this is impossible, repay relatives, or give the money to the needy, or the Church.

Those who have willfully tarnished the good reputation of another must attempt to restore the good name of that individual. The priest will counsel the penitent if restitution is to be made for their sins. Ill-gotten goods never bring happiness.

Contrition

The Council of Trent defines *contrition* as "...sorrow and detestation for sin committed, with a purpose of sinning no more."[267] Jesus told Mary Magdalene to go and sin no more. Those who go to confession need to follow this admonition. People may fall through weakness, but a person who makes no effort and refuses to avoid occasions of sin is not really sorry.

Perfect contrition is sorrow for having offended God. *Imperfect contrition* is sorrow for sin out of fear of going to Hell. Either suffices for validly receiving the Sacrament of Penance.

Perfect contrition is based on love of God, not merely saving one's soul from Hell. A person should always try to have perfect contrition when going to confession. Love of God then becomes the motivating force in striving for virtue and overcoming temptation.

Free Will

God created all human beings with an eternal destiny. Each year, month, week, hour, minute, and second is a gift of God. The joys and pleasures of life are short-lived and shallow. The world cannot give perfect happiness because souls are destined for Heaven.

---

[267] Sess. xiv, De Poenit. cap. 4. can. 5; Sess. vi, xiv.

People have a choice to either love God, obey the Ten Commandments and lead a virtuous life or live a life of self-love, pride and self-gratification and never achieve happiness here or hereafter. To merit Heaven one must be baptized, love God and neighbor, obey the Ten Commandments, and die in the state of grace.

Confessing to God's Representative

Many non-Catholics despise confession since they say they can confess their sins directly to God. A person confessing sins to God receives no assurance that his or her sins are forgiven.

Priests and bishops have been given a divine mission of working for the salvation of souls. They are God's ambassadors who forgive sin by the command and with the power of Christ.

Proper Procedure Before and During Confession

1) Examination of Conscience

An individual needs to review the Ten Commandments, Laws of the Church and duties of one's state of life in order to see how he or she has offended God by sin. This can be done at home or in a pew before going to confession.

2) Sorrow for Sin

A person must hate sin and be sorry for all sins committed.

3) Firm Purpose of Amendment

One must be willing to avoid and remove all occasions of sin.

4) Tell One's Sins Truthfully to the Priest

Give the number of sins, kind of sins and any circumstances that affected them. When an individual is finished say: *I am sorry for these and all the sins of my past especially...* Then name a sin of the past for which he or she is sorry. This shows repentance and tells the priest that their confession is finished.

5) Listen to the Advice the Priest Gives

He is God's representative and wants to help.

6) Pray the Act of Contrition

Once told to do so by the priest. He will then give absolution.

7) Perform The Penance the Priest Gives the Penitent

These prayers or good works repair for sins and replaces suffering in Purgatory for venial sins or the eternal fires of Hell for mortal sins.

Getting the Most Out of Each Confession

The better one's dispositions are, the more graces an individual receives from each confession and the more temporal punishment (Purgatory time) is removed. It is a good practice to first say all mortal sins in order not to omit them later out of fear.

Some parishes reserve a pew in the back of church for those going to confession while others form a line. There is usually a card with an examination of conscience to assist penitents. Lights indicate that someone is in the confessional and the priest is hearing confessions. A sign with the name of the priest often hangs from his door.

Pastors often invite other priests to hear confessions during Advent, Lent and missions in order to give their flock the opportunity to go to confession to another priest in case people are uncomfortable confessing their sins to a particular priest. This helps both parishes.

Sound travels so penitents need to speak in a low tone of voice in the confessional. If a person overhears the sins of another, he or she is bound never to reveal that information to others.

Most confessionals are like three small closets with kneelers on each side of the priest who is seated in the middle. The priest has sliding doors that connects to the side confessionals and allows him to hear one confession at a time.

When receiving the Sacrament of Penance, be calm and confess sins truthfully. The penitent needs to tell the priest how many times each sin was committed and any circumstances that may change the gravity of the offense. If the priest needs a clarification, he will ask the person to explain.

If one doubts whether something is sinful or not, ask the priest. He is there to listen, guide, forgive, and encourage. Don't rush a confession; also don't go into unnecessary details.

Once a person commits a mortal sin, he or she loses all merits from their actions and the individual becomes an enemy of God. One who dies unrepentant will be eternally separated from God. The Sacrament of Penance restores all merits a person has acquired and reunites that individual to the friendship of God.

How to Go to Confession

After entering the confessional, kneel down, make the Sign of the Cross and say:

Bless me, Father, for I have sinned. My last confession was_____(weeks or months ago).

If this is the first confession, say:
Bless me, Father, for I have sinned. This is my first confession.

Then tell the priest your sins and how many times you have committed them. When you have finished confessing your sins say:

I am sorry for these and all the sins of my past, especially (then mention a sin you are sorry for that you have already confessed).

The priest will talk to you and give you a penance (some prayers) and will tell you to say the Act of Contrition.

Then say the Act of Contrition while the priest recites prayers in Latin (absolution) to forgive your sins. When the priest has finished, return to your place and say the prayers given to you for your penance.

Be Prepared

It is a good practice for individuals and families to pray the Act of Contrition every night before retiring. This prayer asks God for pardon and helps familiarize children and adults with the prayer recited in the confessional when the priest gives absolution. Parents need to spend a few minutes explaining the meaning of the words for their little ones, especially those preparing for their first confession and First Holy Communion.

The Act of Contrition

O my God, I am heartily sorry for having offended Thee, and I detest all my sins, because I dread the loss of Heaven and the pains of Hell, but most of all because they offend Thee, my God, Who art all good and deserving of all my love. I firmly resolve, with the help of Thy grace, to confess my sins, to do penance and to amend my life. Amen.

Additional Information

If a person honestly forgot to confess a mortal sin, the sin is forgiven and the individual may receive Holy Communion but must confess the sin if it comes to mind again.

Reception of the Sacrament of Penance must be accompanied by true repentance and amendment of life. The confessional is not a revolving door that justifies sin; it fortifies one to avoid sin and practice a life of virtue.

An individual must do everything necessary to always remain in the state of grace and prepare for death since God gives each person only so many years and days on earth. Once death occurs, there is no second chance.

Do What is Right

Amendment of Life can be summarized in a few words:

1) Make time to pray daily. This will give grace and inner strength.

2) Don't complain—most people don't listen anyway. Just do what is necessary for salvation.

3) Don't judge others—pray for them. Each person will have enough to answer for at death.

4) Forgive injuries. God forgives sinners in proportion as they forgive others.

5) Don't hold grudges. Only God is perfect. He is patient. Follow His example.

6) Be kind. Say a kind word, lend a helping hand and assist when possible.

7) Never retaliate. It only perpetuates hatred.

8) Don't hoard. Once one's needs are filled, share with others.

9) Be pure in heart, word and mind. Avoid anything that could tarnish purity.

10) Trust God. He knows what He is doing.

11) Attend Mass every Sunday and Holy Day. It draws down immense blessings.

12) Go to Confession and Holy Communion frequently. These give countless graces.

13) Be generous with God. Repay His blessings by leading a good life and inspiring others.

Father, Physician and Judge

When the priest says: *I absolve you from your sins,* he forgives sin in the name of Christ and with the power of Christ that was given him at ordination. Priests are commissioned by God to help guide souls to Heaven and are therefore given the title: *Father.*

Priests fulfill the office of a spiritual father when they forgive sins, guide, encourage, and pray for penitents who come to confession. St. Paul considered himself a spiritual father when he wrote, "For in Christ Jesus, through the gospel, did I beget you."[268]

Priests act like a *spiritual physician* by removing the cancer of sin and replacing it with sanctifying grace and peace of soul. Priests perform the office of *judge* when they take God's place and forgive repentant sinners.

Scriptural Quotes / Writings from the Saints

"...add not sin upon sin." (Ecclesiasticus 5, 5)

"In all thy works remember thy last end." (Ecclesiasticus 7, 40)

"Delay not to be converted to the Lord, and defer it not from day to day. For His wrath shall come on a sudden, and in the time of vengeance He will destroy thee." (Ecclesiasticus 5, 8-9)

"Return to Me, and I will return to you, saith the Lord of Hosts." (Malachias 3, 7)

"I will forgive their iniquity, and I will remember their sin no more." (Jeremias 31, 34)

"Be penitent, therefore, and be converted, that your sins may be blotted out." (Acts 3, 19)

"I have blotted out thy iniquities as a cloud and thy sins as a mist: return to Me; for I have redeemed thee." (Isaias 44, 22)

"My son, hast thou sinned? Do so no more: but for thy former sins also pray that they may be forgiven thee." (Ecclesiasticus 21, 1)

"If your sins be as scarlet, they shall be made as white as snow: and if they be red as crimson, they shall be white as wool." (Isaias 1, 18)

"If the wicked do penance for all his sins which he hath committed, and keep all My commandments, and do judgment and justice, living he shall live, and shall not die." (Ezechiel 18, 21)

"My son, in thy sickness neglect not thyself, but pray to the Lord, and He shall heal thee. Turn away from sin, and order thy hands aright, and cleanse thy heart from all offense." (Ecclesiasticus 38, 9, 13)

St. Gregory relates that although God will pardon penitents, He has not promised sinners tomorrow. Eternity is nothing to be taken lightly. St. Charles Borromeo said, "Forget everything and everybody else, and think only of your own soul."[269]

St. Ambrose simply describes the Sacrament of Penance:

> Confession delivers the soul from death. Confession opens the door to Heaven. Confession brings us hope of salvation. Because of this the Scripture says 'First tell thy iniquities, that you may be justified.' ... For true repentance is grief of heart and sorrow of soul because of the evils a man has committed. True repentance causes us to grieve over our offenses... with the firm intention of never committing them again.[270]

---

[268] 1 Corinthians 4, 15.
[269] Very Rev. Charles Callan, *Illustrations for Sermons and Instructions*, p. 209.
[270] Migne's *Patrologiae Cursus Completus, Series Latina*, 17, Sermon 25. Serm. 9 for Lent, Edition Paris 1844-1866.

The Devil's Favorite Traps

Although devils have had centuries of practice in their attempts to lead souls to Hell, their temptations can be summarized quite simply. They often tell people:

1) It's only a venial sin.

Every sin offends God and merits punishment in this life or the next. Venial sins often lead to mortal sins.

One needs to detest all sin because it offends God and hurts the individual and often others.

2) Everyone else is doing it. It can't be wrong.

It doesn't matter what anyone else is doing. Each person has a free will and there is no excuse when someone does something known to be sinful. At death, God will judge each person individually. At the General Judgment, each person stands alone. Those who knew better or encouraged others to sin will be more severely punished.

3) I might as well commit a few more mortal sins because I have to go to confession anyway.

This mindset caused many of Our Lord's terrible sufferings during His Passion. God is not mocked. He won't forgive those who are not sorry and show no sign of repentance. It is difficult to detest sin after it has ruled one's life. It is foolish to wait until the end to be contrite for sin. A person may not get the chance to go to confession before death.

After a serious fall, one needs to return to God in prayer, break away from occasions of sin and go to confession as soon as possible. This will give the penitent God's forgiveness and special graces to do good and avoid evil in the future.

4) I am a hypocrite and will have to go to confession again.

Everyone is weak, but the Sacrament of Penance gives spiritual strength to help one do good and avoid evil. Our Lord instituted the sacrament to help individuals stay close to Him and remain humble as His dear children, not to be self-centered and proud.

5) I can't confess that.

Priests have heard almost everything and will never be shocked at sins confessed. They are there to listen and assist, like a doctor who monitors a person's symptoms. If one doesn't confess his or her sins in the anonymous confessional protected by the confessional seal, he or she will have all their sins manifested to the entire world at the General Judgment at the End of the World.

6) I am not going to go to confession because I am afraid of what the priest might think.

Doctors try to help people regain or maintain good physical health. Priests want penitents to have their sins forgiven, regain peace of soul and start anew. Dedicated doctors and priests want the best for those they serve. Priests don't remember the sins they have heard and can never reveal anything heard in the confessional. Priests are edified when a person has returned to God and try to do their utmost to assist the individual going to confession.

7) There is no hope. I am going to go to Hell anyway.

People usually feel remorse after they have sinned. Demons try to make sinners feel that God has abandoned them and that there is no hope of improvement. They are liars who only want people to lose their immortal souls and spend eternity in Hell with them.

God will always forgive one who is sincerely sorry and truly repentant.

A Bad Confession

If one purposely conceals or leaves out a mortal sin in confession, the person commits a mortal sin of sacrilege and none of the sins are forgiven.

In order to repair for a bad confession an individual must:

- Tell the priest that you made a bad confession.

- Say the sin or sins you left out.

- Tell the priest the sacraments you received since then.

- Confess any other mortal sins, if you have committed any since your last good confession.

Presumption

It is important never to put off one's conversion since time often runs out before a person has a chance to repent. St. Paul writes: "Behold, now is the acceptable time. Now is the day of salvation!"[271]

During the reign of King Henry VIII of England there was a nobleman who led a sinful life, but presumed on God's mercy. He told St. Thomas More that all he had to do was say three simple words when he was dying, "Lord, pardon me." The saint warned him that such presumption put him in danger of losing his immortal soul, but this had little effect.

As the man was one day crossing a bridge over a swollen river, his horse became frightened and plunged into the raging waters. The rider, who cursed the horse with the words, "May the devil…" was never seen again.

---

[271] 2 Corinthians 6, 2.

Chapter Thirty

The Holy Eucharist

Jesus Christ described the Holy Eucharist to His Apostles and a crowd in Capharnaum.

> I am the Bread of Life. Your fathers ate manna in the desert, and have died. This is the bread that comes down from Heaven, so that if anyone eat of it he will not die. I am the living bread that has come down from Heaven. If anyone eat of this bread he shall live forever; and the bread that I will give is My Flesh for the life of the world.[272]

Our Lord showed the importance of reception of this sacrament when He said:

> Amen, amen I say to you, unless you eat the Flesh of the Son of Man, and drink His Blood you shall not have life in you. He who eats My Flesh and drinks My Blood has life everlasting and I will raise him up on the last day.[273]

The Real Presence of Jesus in the Holy Eucharist

The *Baltimore Catechism* defines the *Holy Eucharist as the sacrament that contains the Body, Blood, Soul, and Divinity of Jesus Christ under the appearances of bread and wine.*[274] The Council of Trent declares that

> ...in the precious [almo][275] sacrament of the Holy Eucharist, after the consecration of the bread and wine, our Lord Jesus Christ, true God and true man, is truly, really and substantially contained under the species of those sensible things.[276]

Real Presence of Jesus in the Holy Eucharist is a proof of God's infinite love and one of the Catholic Faith's greatest mysteries. The Greek work *eucharist* means *to give thanks*.

Transubstantiation

Jesus changed bread and wine into his Body, Blood, Soul, and Divinity at the Last Supper and gave It to His Apostles. In order to perpetuate this event until the end of time, He gave the Apostles and their successors—the popes, bishops and priests of the Catholic Church, the power to affect this same miracle.

Transubstantiation is the word that describes the instantaneous change of the substance of the bread and wine into the Body and Blood of Christ that occurs during the Consecration of the Mass. The accidents (traits) such as the color, shape and taste of the bread and wine remain, but the substance is destroyed and replaced by Jesus Christ.

The Consecration of the Bread and Wine occur during the Canon of the Mass. It begins with the *Sanctus* and ends with the prayer *Per Ipsum* just before the Our Father. The Greek word *canon* means *fixed rule*.

Prefigurements of the Holy Eucharist

The manna in the desert that descended from Heaven and nourished the Chosen People was a prefigurement of the Holy Eucharist. Our Lord performed several miracles to prepare His followers for this sacrament. Jesus multiplied loaves and fishes on two occasions and changed water into wine, a physical impossibility.

---

[272] John 6, 48-52.
[273] John 6, 54-55.
[274] Rev. Thomas Kinkead, *Baltimore Catechism, No. 4*, p. 197.
[275] Literally: nourishing.
[276] Session XIII.

When individuals receive the Holy Eucharist it is called *Holy Communion*. The word *communion* is derived from two Latin words that mean *union with*. At each Holy Communion a person is physically united with Jesus Christ.

Why Did Jesus Institute The Holy Eucharist?

Christ changed bread and wine into His Body, Blood, Soul, and Divinity and perpetuated this miracle through His Church so He could be united with His children, received into their hearts and souls, and remain in tabernacles worldwide. This allows individuals to receive Our Lord, love Him, come to Him with their problems, thank Him, petition Him, tell Him they are sorry for their sins, and talk to Him.

Each Holy Communion resembles Christmas since it is an opportunity to hold Our Lord in one's heart and soul and spend time with Him. At Holy Communion, a person has Christ all to himself and doesn't have to share Him with anyone.

Effects of Devoutly Receiving Holy Communion

The Holy Eucharist *gives sanctifying grace, special sacramental graces, unites the recipient with Christ, invigorates the soul, remits venial sins, and gives one strength to help overcome temptation.*

Requisites for Receiving Holy Communion

To receive Holy Communion *a person must be a baptized Catholic, in the state of grace* (have no mortal sins on the soul), *observe the communion fast,* and *have the right intention* (to receive Holy Communion because that person loves God, not just because everyone else is going).

The Communion Fast

- One may not eat, or drink alcoholic beverages for *three hours* before receiving Communion.

- A person cannot drink anything for *one hour* before reception of Holy Communion.

- Water and necessary medicine may be taken *anytime*.

Reception of Holy Communion

When receiving Holy Communion, go to the altar rail and place your hands under the linen cloth if one is draped over it. Once the person next to you has received Communion, tilt your head back, open your mouth and stick out your tongue, keeping it straight so the Host doesn't fall off. The priest will then place the Host on your tongue while saying the words: "May the Body of Our Lord Jesus Christ preserve your soul unto life everlasting. Amen."

Never chew the Host. Swallow It as soon as it is moist enough. If the Sacred Host sticks to the roof of the mouth, never touch It, but use the tongue to assist in swallowing the Host.

Guidelines

- Someone who has venial sins on the soul may receive Holy Communion.

- A person may never receive Holy Communion if he or she has an unforgiven mortal sin on the soul. The person must go to confession first.

- An individual who feels like vomiting should never receive Holy Communion.

- One who has not observed the communion fast should not receive Holy Communion.

Prayers of the Mass

The Holy Sacrifice of the Mass contains numerous prayers found from the Canon to the Communion Prayers that describe the blessings received from attendance and from reception of Holy Communion. The prayers ask for graces for oneself, one's family and friends, for the good of one's soul, and deliverance from harm. It is also a petition for one to be filled with every grace and heavenly blessing and reach Heaven, a place of comfort, light and peace.

Thanksgiving after Receiving Holy Communion

Jesus stays in one's heart for about 15 minutes after a person receives Holy Communion. Therefore, it is important to focus on what is happening—speak to Our Lord, offer Him your love, petition Christ for your spiritual and physical needs, pray for all your loved ones and the Faithful Departed, tell Him you are sorry for your sins, and talk to Jesus.

Use this time well. Don't waste it by looking at others or being distracted. Don't rush out of church quickly after Mass. Spend a few moments to complete a thanksgiving. The time when Jesus reposes in one's heart is the most precious of the day.

Many say the Prayer before the Crucifix after Communion with an Our Father, Hail Mary and Glory Be. This offers a plenary indulgence under the usual conditions.

First Holy Communion

Those planning on making their First Holy Communion must have attained the age of reason,[277] be able to distinguish the Holy Eucharist from regular bread and make a proper thanksgiving. The person needs to understand what has been covered in this chapter including information about the communion fast and how to make a thanksgiving. The Sacrament of Penance is customarily received before making First Communion.

An individual also needs to know basic Catholic beliefs including the Blessed Trinity, how to properly make the Sign of the Cross, the Ten Commandments, Laws of the Church, and the Holy Days of Obligation.[278] The person should know the Apostles Creed, how to go to confession and memorize the Act of Contrition. On the day of First Holy Communion, boys wear a suit and tie and girls a white dress and veil. At the communion rail, they hold a candle that symbolizes their love for Jesus.

Easter Duty

The Catholic Church commands the faithful who have made their First Holy Communion to receive Holy Communion during Easter time under the pain of mortal sin. This period, in the United States, extends from the First Sunday of Lent until Trinity Sunday.

The Easter Duty also includes going to confession once a year. This period extends from January 1 to December 31. If one does not fulfill this serious obligation, that person is not considered to be a practicing Catholic and the Church forbids ecclesiastical burial.

---

[277] "Age of Reason, the name given to that period of human life at which persons are deemed to begin to be morally responsible." *Catholic Encyclopedia Vol. 1*, p. 209.

[278] The book *The Family Catechism* wonderfully adapts Catholic beliefs to the mind of a child especially in these areas. It is available from stjosephsmedia.com.

Holy Viaticum

Holy Communion presented to a person for the last time is called Holy Viaticum—"food for the journey." The priest uses the following form for the sacrament for a dying person: "Receive brother (sister), the Viaticum of the Body of Our Lord Jesus Christ, that He may guard you from the malignant enemy (the devil) and lead you into eternal life. Amen."[279]

From Time into Eternity

As life fades and judgment looms, many desire to make their peace with God. Everyone desires a tranquil death, but one must use the means necessary to achieve it.

When death is imminent, everyone wants to have family and close friends nearby. What greater friend is there than Our Lord Who died on the Cross in order to redeem and save souls?

What a consolation at death for Jesus to enter a person's heart and soul! Since the journey to eternity begins with the Particular Judgment at the time of passing, reception of the Sacrament of Penance and Holy Viaticum allows individuals to renew their friendship with God. What a blessed way to enter eternity!

Final Perseverance

Catholics recite the words, "Pray for us sinners, now and at the hour of our death" every time they pray the Hail Mary. These are some of the most important words they will ever say. St. Francis of Assisi said as wax disappears before fire and dust is scattered by the wind, so the entire army of evil spirits flees at the simple invocation of the name of Mary.

Final perseverance is the special gift of God by which one dies in the state of sanctifying grace. St. Augustine teaches that "God grants final perseverance only to those who ask Him for it."[280] It is imperative to pray daily for a holy and happy death.

A Sacrilegious Communion

A Catholic may *never* go to Holy Communion in the state of mortal sin. This is a sacrilege and a very serious sin. In order to have mortal sin(s) forgiven, an individual must go to confession.

Parishioners should *never judge* those not receiving Holy Communion since some individuals may have received communion at an earlier Mass or not fulfilled the communion fast. Catholics may only receive Holy Communion once a day.

Seeing with the Eyes of Faith

A great miracle once occurred during the reign of King Louis IX (St. Louis) of France. Jesus appeared radiantly from the Sacred Host in a church in Paris.

Multitudes flocked to see this proof of the Real Presence of Jesus in the Holy Eucharist. The king was requested to view the marvel, but said he didn't need to go since his faith already allowed him to see what others viewed with their eyes.

---

[279] *Accipe frater (soror), Viaticum Corpus Domini nostri Jesu Christi, qui te custodiat ab hoste maligno, et perducat in vitam aeternum. Amen.*

[280] Benedictine Convent of Perpetual Adoration, Clyde, Missouri, *Prayer: the Great Means of Grace,* p. 10.

Chapter Thirty-One

Confirmation

The Apostles were cowardly before Pentecost. Peter denied knowing Christ. The others were afraid they might be crucified like Jesus. After Pentecost, they became changed men.

The Catechism of the Council of Trent demonstrated the far-reaching effects of Confirmation by noting that once the Holy Ghost came upon the Apostles, the timid fishermen were transformed into valiant missionaries who traversed the globe and converted many to Christ.

A Powerful Sacrament

Confirmation is the sacrament by which the Holy Ghost comes to the recipient in a special manner and enables that person to become a spiritually strong and mature[281] Christian. It also helps one profess the faith as a soldier of Jesus Christ. The person who is confirmed chooses to remain on God's side and combat the world, fallen human nature, and the devil that wars against God.

In order to receive the Sacrament of Confirmation, a person must be baptized, in the state of grace and know the basic tenets of the Catholic Faith.

Effects of Confirmation

Confirmation gives the recipient the Seven Gifts of the Holy Ghost, strengthens one's faith, gives an increase of sanctifying grace, and imprints a permanent seal on the soul.

The Seven Gifts of the Holy Ghost

Wisdom	puts life into perspective allowing one to see things the way God does.
Understanding	gives a person a deeper grasp of the faith to distinguish truth from error.
Counsel	guides an individual to make the right decisions.
Fortitude	gives spiritual strength to keep the commandments and lead a virtuous life.
Knowledge	assists one to understand God's goodness and the value of the soul.
Piety	helps a person grow in love of God and neighbor.
Fear of the Lord	inspires an individual with a reverential fear of offending God.

The Gifts of the Holy Ghost are infused into the soul. The more they are utilized, the closer one is drawn to God and holiness. Pope Leo XIII wrote: "These gifts of the Holy Ghost are of such efficacy that they lead the confirmed Christian to the very summit of holiness."[282]

Permanent Seal on the Soul

There are three sacraments that place a permanent seal (mark) on the soul—Baptism, Confirmation and Holy Orders. Therefore, they can be received only once. In Heaven, these marks will be a source of glory.

---

[281] The graces received help one develop a deeper interior life and closer union with God.
[282] *Divinum Illud Munus*, 1897.

The Twelve Fruits of the Holy Ghost

The fruits of the Holy Ghost are present in one who has received Confirmation and cooperates with the special graces of the sacrament.

Charity, Joy, Peace, Patience

Goodness, Kindness[283] **Mildness**

Modesty, Chastity, Continency

Long Suffering[284] **and Faith**[285]

The opposite vices will often be present in one who is not practicing the Faith.

The Confirmation Ceremony

The rite often begins with the chanting of the *Veni Sancte Spiritus*, although this is not of obligation. The bishop then recites prayers asking that the Holy Ghost come upon those being confirmed, that the power of the Most High guard them from sin and for the confirmed to receive the Seven Gifts of the Holy Ghost.

At the beginning of the rite, the person being confirmed is addressed by the bishop, who uses the Latin vocative form of the name chosen by the *confirmandi*.[286] Those being confirmed choose a Confirmation name of a saint they would like to imitate and have as a special heavenly patron.

The bishop then places his right hand on the head of the *confirmandi* and anoints the forehead with Holy Chrism[287] while reciting the form of the sacrament after which the server answers, *Amen*. The bishop or server wipes excess oil from the forehead after each anointing.

The bishop then says, *Pax tecum* (peace be with you) while administering a slight slap to the cheek of the person being confirmed. This is done in order to remind the individual to live the Catholic Faith and be willing, if necessary, to suffer and die for Christ.

Pope Pius XI said soldiers of Christ who are engaged in a spiritual combat should not focus solely on personal sanctification, but should also strive to save others souls. St. Hippolytus described Confirmation in his work *Apostolic Tradition*.[288] The *Gelasian Sacramentary* of the ninth century gives the form of the sacrament that is used today.

Confirmation Sponsors

A Confirmation sponsor must be a baptized Catholic who was previously confirmed, knows the basic beliefs of the Faith, is 14 years of age or older,[289] and of the same sex as the person being confirmed.

---

[283] Also called *Benignity*. Fr. Faber said that supernatural "kindness has converted more sinners than zeal, eloquence or learning and these three things have never converted anybody without kindness having something to do with it."
　　Dom J. Chautard, OCR, The *Soul of the Apostolate,* pp. 128-129.
[284] To patiently bear adversity.
[285] Fidelity to God.
[286] Person about to be confirmed.
[287] Holy Chrism symbolizes spiritual strength and a good life.
[288] Third century, p. 22.
[289] Unless there is a good reason.

A parent or spouse cannot be a sponsor and a sponsor used at Baptism cannot be used as a Confirmation sponsor.

During the Confirmation ceremony, the sponsor stands behind the person being confirmed and holds a card with the Confirmation name[290] of the individual in the left hand while placing the right hand on the right shoulder of the individual as he or she receives the sacrament.

Closing Ceremonies

The bishop then washes his hands with lemon,[291] bread, cotton, and water, as the choir sings an antiphon (hymn) *Confirmo hoc Deus*. The bishop then says a closing prayer, gives a blessing and speaks to those who have been confirmed and their sponsors. The confirmed are then asked to stand and recite the Apostles Creed, Our Father and Hail Mary.

The Visit of the Bishop

The annual visit of the bishop is a special event for each parish. He is a successor of the Apostles and should be shown the respect due to his elevated office. Bishops are addressed by the phrase *your excellency*. It is customary to kiss the bishop's ring when greeting him[292] and before receiving Holy Communion.

Symbols of the Bishop's Office and Authority

A number of symbols represent the bishop's office. These include his episcopal ring, miter, staff (crozier), pectoral cross, skullcap (zucchetto), Roman purple sash, and shoulder cape. The bishop's crozier is shaped like a shepherd's staff to symbolize leading souls entrusted to his care and retrieving those who have wandered or strayed.

A Sacrament of Spiritual Maturity

Since most Catholics are baptized as infants, Confirmation is an external acknowledgement of an individual's acceptance of the Catholic Faith and all it entails. Sponsors renounced Satan for those baptized as infants and made acts of faith for them in the Blessed Trinity. At Confirmation, *confirmandi* come to the communion rail of their own volition.

They personally choose their Confirmation name, are anointed on the forehead, receive the imposition of the bishop's hands and recite prayers aloud when requested to do so. They receive a sacrament that will assist them for years to come.

The Importance of Confirmation Today

In an age that has rejected God and mocks religion, it is more important than ever for young Catholics to receive this sacrament to help them practice and defend the Faith and explain it to others. The Gifts of the Holy Ghost remain for life and should be utilized daily.

---

[290] Written in the Latin vocative form so the bishop can read it during the ceremony.
[291] To remove what remains of the Holy Chrism.
[292] Those who are able customarily genuflect on the left knee while doing so.

Extraordinary Minister in Danger of Death

In accordance with a Decree of the Congregation of the Sacraments, dated 14th September, 1946, and taking effect on 1st January 1947, parish priests or their equivalent (not, however, their curates or assistants) are empowered by a general indult of the Holy See to administer this Sacrament [Confirmation], as extraordinary ministers, to the faithful within their own territory when they are truly in danger of death by sickness, and when the bishop of the diocese or other bishop in communion with the Holy See, is not available. The reason of this measure is to ensure that the grace of Confirmation, which though not necessary for salvation, is yet of great spiritual profit to the soul and a means of greater glory in Heaven, may not be denied to the many infants, children and adults who, being in danger of death by sickness might never be able to obtain it if the Church insisted upon the exact observance of the common law in regard to the ordinary minister of this Sacrament.[293]

---

[293] *Acta Apostolicae Sedis* XXXVIII, 1946, pp. 349-358.

Chapter Thirty-Two
Matrimony

After God created Adam, the first man in the Garden of Paradise, He said: "It is not good for man to be alone: let us make him a helpmate like unto himself."[294] God then created Eve, established the institution of marriage and blessed Adam and Eve saying: "Increase and multiply and fill the earth."[295] Marriage affects every facet of society.

The primary purpose of marriage is the generation and education of children. The secondary purpose is mutual love and help, and assistance against concupiscence.

Children are greatly affected by their surroundings. If parents are loving, caring and devout, the children often follow their parents' example. If parents are distant, uncaring, lax, and irreligious, the children may mirror their behavior.

Marriage Raised to the Level of a Sacrament

Jesus performed His first public miracle at a wedding reception in Cana of Galilee and elevated the lifelong marital contract to the dignity of a sacrament. Matrimony bestows special sacramental graces upon married couples to fulfill their obligations and assist them in effecting the salvation of their souls and those of their children. These graces include to love and remain faithful to each other, properly raise a family, lovingly care for their children and perseveringly perform the sacrifices necessary to preserve domestic tranquility.

Matrimony is the sacrament that unites a baptized man and baptized woman for life and grants them all the graces necessary to preserve that union and required for the proper raising and education of their children. The Sacrament of Matrimony is extremely important today because it provides stability to families and society. "What therefore God has joined together, let no man put asunder." (Mark 10, 9)

Marriage is attacked on all sides today. Satan attempts to destroy the family by loose morals, society's acceptance of abortion, adultery, artificial birth control, divorce, homosexual and lesbian lifestyles, indecent fashions, pornography, and premarital sex.

Sex is a power given to husband and wife to show love for one another and to bring life into the world. Matrimony and valid marriage legitimize the use of this power. It helps the couple stay together for life and assists children conceived by the union to receive love and proper care.

Marrying a Catholic

Catholics are bound by Church law to marry another Catholic. They are happier than couples with little or no faith since they are united in a common bond and have like aspirations. Since they both view life the same way, religion is a blessing, not a point of contention. Good Catholic parents attend Mass on all Sundays and Holy Days, frequent the Sacraments of Penance and Holy Eucharist, have their children baptized and engage in family prayer.

Catholic couples reinforce the faith of their children who feel content and undivided since both parents have the same beliefs and abide by the same laws. Many Catholic marriages last for life since they are not allowed to divorce and can only remarry after the death of a spouse.

---

[294] Genesis 2, 18.
[295] Genesis 1, 28.

Marrying a Non-Catholic

The Church occasionally grants a dispensation that allows a Catholic to marry a non-Catholic. The dispensation for *mixed religion* may be given if a Catholic marries a baptized non-Catholic. The dispensation for *disparity of cult* may be given if a Catholic marries a non-baptized person.

Before giving the dispensation, the priest or bishop must be assured that the non-Catholic will allow the Catholic and the children the free exercise of their faith. There should also be good hope for conversion.

Matrimonial Promises

To protect the Catholic spouse and the children born of the union, the Church demands that both Catholic and non-Catholic spouses sign a formal guarantee—an oath. The Catholic must swear to God that he or she will practice the Catholic religion, baptize the children Catholic and raise them in the Faith. The non-Catholic must swear to allow the Catholic spouse and children to live the Catholic Faith and that the children will be baptized Catholic. It is important for the Catholic spouse to fearlessly live the faith and not cater to human respect. This will inspire the non-Catholic who may convert by the good example given.

Dangers

Many Catholics have lost their faith after marrying non-Catholics since it is easy to disregard the commandments and neglect to go to church. Children often take the easy route and often end up with no religion. Sadly, this cycle is perpetuated for generations.

Some foolishly believe that *they* will convert their spouse. It doesn't happen that way. God's grace effects conversions and an individual must be open-minded and have a good will. People are creatures of habit and upbringing affects the way a person thinks and acts.

Good Example

The Catholic spouse needs to give good example since more are converted by example and prayer than words. Sometimes non-Catholic spouses convert and become fervent Catholics.

It is a good sign when the non-Catholic is open to the Catholic Faith and / or attends Mass with the Catholic. This is a sign of love and will make the marriage more tranquil.

The Marriage Ceremony

The wedding ceremony between a Catholic and a non-Catholic consists in the bridesmaids and bride entering, the wedding vows, placement of rings by groom and bride, and an exhortation at the beginning and end of the ceremony. No Mass is offered, the couple does not receive the Nuptial Blessing and priestly vestments are not worn. The vows bind for life and neither party can remarry while their spouse is alive.

Preparation for Marriage

The priest meets and holds classes with couples interested in getting married. Topics discussed include the sanctity of marriage, mutual obligations to each other, responsibilities to subsequent children, importance of practicing virtue and avoiding occasions of sin, various aspects of married life, the need to work together, proper raising of children, respecting one another, the four temperaments, overcoming bad habits and addictions, financial planning, and a brief review of the Catholic Faith if needed. Practical details about preparing for the wedding are given and a fixed date and time are set for the special event.

The couple is reminded that marriage is sacred. Therefore, the attire of the bride and bridesmaids must be modest since the event takes place in church. The party to be married are often given a copy of the marriage vows in order to familiarize themselves with the wording.

A practice is scheduled usually the evening before the wedding and conducted by the priest with the couple, parents, bridal party, and organist in attendance. The priest customarily hears the confessions of the future bride and groom after the practice.

The Sacrament of Matrimony

The rite begins with an exhortation reminding the couple of the sacredness and seriousness of the marital union. Positive and negative elements of life are described to the couple as well as the need to love one another and be willing to sacrifice in order to preserve their lifelong bond.

No greater blessing can come to your married life than pure conjugal love, loyal and true to the end. May, then, this love with which you join your hands and hearts today, never fail, but grow deeper and stronger as the years go on. And if true love and the unselfish spirit of perfect sacrifice guide your every action, you can expect the greatest measure of earthly happiness that may be allotted to man in this vale of tears. The rest is in the hands of God. Nor will God be wanting to your needs; He will pledge you the life-long support of His graces in the Holy Sacrament which you are now going to receive.[296]

Consent

The priest then asks the groom and bride individually by name if they wish to marry each other according to the rite of Holy Mother Church. Once they answer in the affirmative, the marriage vows are recited while the couple hold right hands.

Marriage Vows / Wedding Rings

Wedding vows are a lifelong contract between husband and wife whereby they give exclusive rights to the other taking their spouse "...for better, for worse, for richer for poorer, in sickness and in health until death do us part." The priest then blesses the couple saying: "I unite you in marriage in the name of the Father and of the Son and of the Holy Ghost. Amen."

Rings are then blessed and placed by the groom and bride on the ring finger of the left hand of their spouse while saying "With this ring I thee wed and I pledge unto thee my fidelity."

Prayer Before Mass

The priest then encourages the married couple to utilize the graces they have received for themselves and their future children. He then blesses them with holy water. The newlyweds then attend Mass on kneelers placed within the sanctuary of the church.

The Nuptial Mass

The Church allows the Nuptial Mass on all feasts of double rank or lower. It is a special Mass, without a Gloria that focuses on the blessing of marriage and the graces bestowed by the Sacrament of Matrimony. The Nuptial Blessing is given to the Catholic bride and groom after the Our Father of the Mass and before the Last Blessing. The first blessing refers especially to the bride, the second to both.

---

[296] Rev. Paul Griffith, *The Priest's New Ritual*, pp. 208-209.

The Nuptial Blessing

This ancient prayer[297] asks God's blessings on the couple and petitions, they see their children's children to the third and fourth generation.

May the God of Abraham, the God of Isaac, and the God of Jacob be with you. May He fulfill His blessing in you so that you may see your children's children even to the third and fourth generation. Afterwards may you have life everlasting, by the assistance of our Lord Jesus Christ, who with the Father and Holy Ghost, liveth and reigneth, God forever and ever. Amen.

Closing Exhortation

Once Mass has ended the priest turns toward the bride and groom and reminds them to be grateful for the graces they have received and reads them part of the Epistle of St. Paul dealing with marriage. Lastly, he prays that their union may lead them to the everlasting union with God in Heaven. The bridal party then exits the church. Often the bride stops by a statue of Mary and prays that Our Lady will assist her to be a good wife and mother before leaving.

Ecclesiastical Laws of Marriage

The two essential qualities of Matrimony are: *unity* and *indissolubility*. *Unity* means that once a person is married the individual cannot have sexual relations with anyone other than their husband or wife. It forbids adultery and dangerous friendships with members of the opposite sex. *Indissolubility* means that the marriage lasts for the life of the bride and groom.

The Church wants to make sure the couple practices the faith and subsequent children born of the union attend Church and receive the sacraments. For the marriage of a Catholic to be valid, it must be performed before a Catholic priest and two witnesses.[298] This ensures that the couple is prepared and that the proper form is used. A Catholic is forbidden to marry close relatives such as uncles, aunts, nieces, nephew, or first or second cousins.

There must be two official witnesses for a wedding called the Best Man and Maid (or Matron) of Honor. In the United States, these do not have to be Catholic. A couple planning on marrying must get a marriage license in the United States within a month of the wedding.

A marriage by a Catholic before a judge or justice of the peace is invalid. If a Catholic contracts marriage before a non-Catholic minister it is invalid and he or she incurs the penalty of excommunication, expulsion from the Catholic Church.

An *annulment* (decree of nullity) is an official ecclesiastical declaration, following careful analysis of the evidence, that a marriage never existed. This can be due to a defective consent or a diriment impediment.[299]

"Separation [from bed and board] is only permitted for a very serious reason and only with the permission of the bishop. A separated person is not allowed to keep company with another person."[300] Grounds for separation include adultery, grave spiritual or bodily danger, cruelty, non-support, and public apostasy. The Council of Trent treats of the matter in Session 24, canon 8 and says the time of separation can be determinate or indeterminate. Hopefully matters can be remedied for the sake of the children and to prevent adultery.

---

[297] Taken in part from blessings given to Adam and Eve (Genesis 27, 27-30) and to Tobias (Tobias 8, 10).
[298] See Council of Trent, Session XXIV, Chapter I.
[299] See Canon George Smith, DD, PhD, *The Teachings of the Catholic Church: Volume Two,* p. 1098.
[300] Parish Priests of Chicago, *Lessons in the Catholic Faith,* p. 78.

Chapter Thirty-Three

Holy Orders

There are a number of steps one must take in order to become a priest including Tonsure and Minor and Major Orders. Seminarians normally spend at least six years in study before ordination. Two years are spent covering the branches of philosophy and four years are spent in Dogmatic Theology, Moral Theology, Canon Law, and Scripture Studies. There are also classes in Latin, Greek, the Liturgy, Homiletics,[301] and other fields.

Those in Major Orders are bound to lifelong celibacy and to the recitation of the Divine Office. The bishop is the only person who can ordain a priest or consecrate another bishop.

Three bishops customarily take part in the solemn ceremony of the Consecration of a Bishop. *Apostolic Succession* is the term describing the direct lineage between a bishop and his predecessor that goes all the way back to the Apostles.

The sacrificing priesthood is a characteristic that distinguishes the Catholic Church from other religions. The men chosen for this sacred profession receive authority and power from Christ to continue His work on earth.

Steps to the Priesthood

Tonsure a seminarian becomes a member of the clergy.

Minor Orders

Porter cares for the church.

Exorcist receives power to perform exorcisms.[302]

Lector chants lessons and blesses first fruits.

Acolyte commissioned to serve Mass.

Major Orders

Subdeacon can sing the Epistle and serve during a Solemn High Mass.

Deacon may solemnly baptize,[303] preach and distribute Holy Communion.

Priest has the power to offer Mass, confect the sacraments[304] and bless.

Bishop possesses the fullness of the priesthood and confers Confirmation and Holy Orders.

Holy Orders is the sacrament that gives a man the graces and powers to serve God as bishop, priests and other ministers of the Church.

The Lifeblood of the Catholic Church

The priesthood is the lifeblood of the Catholic Church. Priests and bishops confect the sacraments, teach the Faith, guide their flocks, protect them from erroneous teachings and dangers, encourage them and attempt to lead them to Heaven. Although priests have many duties their most important role is offering the Holy Sacrifice of the Mass and praying the Divine Office.

---

[301] The art of preaching and giving inspiring, well-prepared sermons.
[302] A priest or cleric who is an exorcist must have his bishop's permission to perform a solemn exorcism.
[303] With permission.
[304] A priest cannot validly ordain others (Holy Orders) and may only confirm as noted in footnote 118.

The Necessity of Priests and Bishops in the Catholic Church

Priests and bishops baptize the new Catholic to remove original sin, offer a soul sanctifying grace for the first time, and make the individual a child of God.

Priests and bishops forgive sin and allow a soul to return to God through the Sacrament of Penance and offer the individual strength and grace to avoid sin in the future.

Priests and bishops offer the Holy Sacrifice of the Mass to honor God, bestow blessings on their flocks and others, and assist the Faithful Departed in Purgatory. By fervent reception of the Holy Eucharist souls are brought closer to God and are assisted on their journey to Heaven.

By Confirmation, bishops bestow on Catholics the Seven Gifts of the Holy Ghost and special graces that will assist them for the rest of their lives. These new soldiers of Christ are strengthened to live and practice their faith and overcome the temptations of the devil.

Matrimony bestows on couples all the graces needed to preserve their lifelong union and also gives them all the spiritual helps necessary to raise a family.

Bishops who confer Holy Orders (ordaining priests and consecrating bishops) ensure that the Catholic Church will be preserved—that there will always be ministers of God who will offer Mass, confect the sacraments and teach Christ's doctrine until the end of time. During the ordination ceremony, the bishop tells the newly ordained priest that whatever he blesses will be blessed, whatever he consecrates will be consecrated and whose sins he forgives, they are forgiven.

Priests and bishops who confer Extreme Unction prepare a soul to enter eternity.

Symbolism of Ceremonies

Ceremonies of the Ordination of a Priest and Consecration of a Bishop symbolize the graces and responsibilities of those sacred offices. The imposition of hands by the bishop on the deacon who becomes a priest and by three bishops on a priest who becomes a bishop symbolizes the authority and power of Christ being transferred to the recipient by Christ's representative. These ceremonies also manifest the hierarchical structure of the Church.

The bishop anoints the hands of a newly ordained priest with Holy Oil to symbolize the sacredness of his calling and mission, especially to offer Mass. The head of a newly consecrated bishop is anointed with Holy Chrism to show that he is chosen by God to rule.

The bishop presents the chalice, paten and host to the newly ordained priest and commands him to offer sacrifice (Mass) for the living and the dead. The consecrating bishop presents the episcopal ring and crozier to the new bishop that he may rule and guard the Catholic Church.

Chapter Thirty-Four

Extreme Unction

Some believe that receiving Extreme Unction (last anointing) may hasten their death. They fail to realize its many benefits and the fact that a great number of recipients who receive it, revive. Yet the sacrament is not to be used as a substitute for necessary medical help.

Extreme Unction is the sacrament that fortifies the soul and often gives health to the body through the prayer and anointing by the priest. All Catholics who have reached the age of reason that are in danger of death through sickness, accident or old age should receive this sacrament.

The sickness or accident must be life threatening. Since it is not a blessing, but a sacrament, Extreme Unction is never to be received more than once a month unless a new condition arises.

Extreme Unction has numerous effects: *It bestows sanctifying grace, removes the temporal punishment due to sin, forgives sins and cleanses the soul. It gives comfort and peace as a person is reassured of God's care. The recipient receives strength against the devil and temptation. Lastly, it prepares one for entrance into Heaven if a person is to die soon afterwards or restores health if it is for the good of the soul.*

To receive these graces, a person needs to be properly disposed. If there is doubt whether the person is still alive before *rigor mortis* sets in, the priest may anoint the individual conditionally.[305]

Ceremonies

The rite begins with the priest saying in Latin: *Peace be to this house to all who dwell therein* while sprinkling those present with holy water in the form of a cross. A crucifix is then presented to the sick person.

The priest then says several prayers asking for heavenly assistance from God and the angels. The room is then blessed with words recited in Latin:

> Hear, us O Lord, Holy Father, Almighty and Eternal God and deign to send thy holy angel from Heaven that he may guard, watch over, protect, and defend all who inhabit this home. Through Christ Our Lord. Amen.

Extreme Unction includes an exorcism prayer recited in Latin. The priest places his hand above the head of the person receiving the sacrament and says:

> May any power that the Devil has over you be utterly destroyed. As I place my hands on you and call on the help of the Glorious and Holy Mother of God, the Virgin Mary, her illustrious spouse, St. Joseph, and all the holy angels, archangels, patriarchs, prophets, Apostles, martyrs, confessors, virgins, and all the saints. Amen.

The priest then anoints the person with Oil of the Sick making the Sign of the Cross over the eyes, ears, nostrils, lips, hands, and feet[306] of the individual saying:

> Through this holy anointing and His holy loving mercy, may the Lord forgive you whatever sins you have committed by the sense of (sight, hearing, smell, taste, speech, touch, and walking). Amen.

---

[305] The form used is: (If you are living) *Si vivis, per istam sanctam Unctionem + indulgeat tibi Dominus quidquid deliquisti. Amen.*
[306] The anointing of the feet is not of obligation and Canon 947 says it may be omitted for any reasonable cause.

The priest then wipes off the excess oil from the senses with cotton using a new one for each sense. He then cleans his thumb and recites three other prayers and the words:

> Is any man sick among you? Let him call in the priests of the Church, and let them pray over him, anointing him with oil in the name of the Lord: and the prayer of faith shall save the sick man, and the Lord will raise him up; and if he be in sins they shall be forgiven him.[307]

Christ instituted Extreme Unction and taught it to the Apostles. There are numerous references to the sacrament including the Acts of the Apostles, the Epistle of St. James, the writings of St. Ambrose (fourth century), and from Pope Innocent I who mentions it in 416 AD. Many of the prayers are found in ancient sacramentaries as well.

The Last Sacraments

The Last Sacraments consist of Penance (Confession), Holy Eucharist (often in the form of Holy Viaticum) and Extreme Unction. These three sacraments prepare a person to enter eternity.

The family should prepare if possible a small table with a crucifix, a pair of candles, a small container of water, and a small spoon.[308] Never light candles if the person is on oxygen.

If possible meet the priest (who comes to the house with the Sacred Host in the pyx around his neck) at the door with a lit candle and lead him to the sick person. The priest will then place the Blessed Sacrament on a white linen cloth called a corporal, say some prayers and bless the room with holy water. Then he will hear the individual's confession. If the person is unconscious, the priest may give conditional absolution.

Holy Communion is given if the dying individual is conscious and able to receive. If death is imminent, the last Communion is known as Holy Viaticum. Those present are asked to pray and the person receives Extreme Unction and Apostolic Blessing unless it was already given.

Deceased practicing Catholics are to receive proper burial in consecrated ground. The body is sacred and was animated by the immortal soul during life.

Never Give Up

Since hearing is believed to be the last sense to go, be careful not to say anything in the presence of a sick person that would cause the individual to panic or despair. A man was once lying in the hospital paralyzed in a state of coma. The doctors said, "He is dying. It is hopeless." A priest who was brought in was told he was too late. The priest didn't care and gave him Extreme Unction and the man miraculously recovered! The doctor attributed this cure to the efficacy of this sacrament.

---

[307] Rev. Paul Griffith, *The Priest's New Ritual*, pp. 32-33, James 5, 14-15.
[308] The priest will have these items in his sick call kit if they are not available from the family.

Chapter Thirty-Five
The Catholic Church

It is a historical fact that Jesus Christ founded the Catholic Church. *This visible Church has a fixed set of beliefs* (the Deposit of Faith: Sacred Scripture and Apostolic Tradition), *a uniform form of worship* (the Holy Sacrifice of the Mass), Seven Sacraments that give grace to the recipients *and a hierarchy* (pope, bishops and priests who minister to the laity).

A Visible Church

Jesus Christ referred to His Church when He spoke of the vine and branches and when He later said: "I am the Good Shepherd. I know mine and mine know Me."[309]

> I am the true Vine, and My Father is the Vine Dresser. Every branch in Me that bears no fruit he will take away; and every branch that bears fruit He will cleanse, that it may bear more fruit.

> I am the Vine, you are the branches. He who abides in Me, and I in him, bears much fruit; for without Me you can do nothing. If anyone does not abide in Me, he shall be cast outside as a branch and wither; and they shall gather them up and cast them into the fire, and they shall burn.[310]

Our Lord founded the Catholic Church. "...thou art Peter; and upon this rock I will build My Church, and the Gates of Hell shall not prevail against it."[311] During the three years of Christ's Public Life He taught the Apostles, disciples and His followers, and later commanded them to fearlessly spread the Catholic Faith throughout the entire world. The Catholic Church has always had a missionary spirit and works to instruct converts around the world since the highest form of charity for others is to work for the eternal salvation of their immortal souls.

Individuals have an obligation to seek the truth found in the Catholic Church. Although everyone has a free will, a person is culpable who remains indifferent or apathetic in religious matters, especially since Jesus Christ came down from Heaven to redeem the world and founded the Catholic Church. Since Our Lord established the Barque of Peter, He expects individuals to step on board. Those who willingly remain away are culpable in His eyes. "He who believes and is baptized shall be saved. He who does not believe shall be condemned."[312]

The Authority of the Catholic Church

The protection and guidance of the Holy Ghost are reflected in the three attributes of the Catholic Church: *authority, infallibility* and *indefectibility*. The Catholic Church was given its *authority* by Jesus Christ its Founder, Who said: "He who hears you, hears Me."[313]

Christ told the Apostles to "teach all nations, baptizing them in the name of the Father, and of the Son, and of the Holy Ghost, teaching them to observe all things whatsoever I have commanded you."[314]

Jesus Christ, Who founded the Catholic Church, gave it His authority whereby Popes rule over the Universal Church, bishops over their dioceses and flocks, and priests over their parishes. The three rings of the papal tiara symbolize that the pope is to teach, rule and sanctify.

---

[309] John 10, 14.
[310] John 15, 5-6.
[311] Matthew 16, 18.
[312] Mark 16, 16.
[313] Luke 10, 16.
[314] Matthew 28, 19-20.

The Hierarchy of the Catholic Church

Our Lord established a hierarchal church with a chain of command and appointed St. Peter, the first pope and His vicar on earth, to rule over the Church. All subsequent legitimate popes[315] are his successors. "...thou art Peter; and upon this rock I will build My Church..."[316] The hierarchy preserves and spreads Christ's teachings, rules their flocks, confects the sacraments, offers the Holy Sacrifice of the Mass, and leads souls to Heaven.

Interregnum

The Church continues to operate when the Chair of Peter is vacant between the reign of popes (*interregnum*) as when it is waiting for a successor to be elected[317] or when there is a doubtful pope. As a case in point, during the Western Schism (1378-1418 AD), three men claimed to be pope. Since the Catholic Church must work unceasingly for the salvation of souls until the end of time, the Church supplies jurisdiction to bishops and priests during a period of *interregnum*.

In the United States of America, once a president dies, the country continues to operate. The same is true of the Catholic Church when a pope dies.

The *Teaching Magisterium*, consisting of the pope and the bishops teaching in union with him, infallibly teaches the doctrines of Christ and makes them available across the globe.

Authority is transferred from Christ, the Head of the Catholic Church to the pope, His vicar on earth, to the bishops often appointed by the pope,[318] to the priests who serve parishes. The Council of Trent (1545–1563 AD) taught that the powers given by Christ to the Apostles are passed on to the bishops.

- The Pope is Christ's vicar on earth
- Bishops possess the fullness of the priesthood to rule over their flocks and dioceses.
- Priests offer the Mass and the sacraments to their parishioners.
- Deacons often assist in parishes while studying to become priests. Famous deacons include St. Francis of Assisi and the martyrs St. Stephen, St. Lawrence and St. Vincent.

Honorary offices in the Church give no additional sacramental powers. *Cardinals* elect popes. *Archbishops* rule over other bishops. *Monsignors* are priests who have been honored by the pope for distinguished service.

Infallibility

The pope is protected by papal infallibility from ever teaching the Universal Church anything contrary to the faith and good morals. When the pope infallibly defines a doctrine, he merely makes a public declaration of what has always been taught by the Church.

Christ provided for the precise transmission of His immutable teachings from age to age by papal infallibility, the divine safeguard that protects popes from teaching heresy in matters of faith and morals. A pope cannot invent new doctrines nor teach anything contrary to the Deposit of Faith. Msgr. Van Noort says, "Infallibility is not merely the absence of error, but the impossibility of erring."[319]

---

[315] There have been 41 antipopes from the years 217-1449.
[316] Matthew 16, 18.
[317] In Latin: *sede vacante.*
[318] This practice is of fairly recent origin due to poor communications and the distance between Rome and a diocese.
[319] *Christ's Church,* p. 119.

Pope Pius XII wrote of the infallibility of papal encyclical (letters) in *Humani Generis:*

> ...if the Supreme Pontiffs in their official documents purposely pass judgment on a matter up to that time under dispute, it is obvious that the matter, according to the mind and will of the same Pontiffs, cannot be any longer considered a question open to discussion among theologians.

The Holy Ghost, the Third Person of the Holy Trinity, the Spirit of Truth protects the pope from teaching error as confirmed by the Vatican Council of 1869-1870 that said:

> ...the Holy Ghost was not promised to the successors of Peter in such a way that, by His revelation they might manifest new doctrine, but so that, by His assistance, they might guard as sacred and might faithfully propose the revelation delivered through the Apostles, or the Deposit of Faith.[320]

Dogma

The Vatican Council of 1869-1870 infallibly declared what one must believe to be a member of the Catholic Church. The theological term used is *de fide* (concerning the faith).

> All those things are to be believed by divine and Catholic faith which are contained in the Word of God written [Sacred Scripture] or handed down [Apostolic Tradition] and which are proposed for our belief by the Church either in a solemn definition or in its ordinary and universal teaching authority.[321]

Dr. Ludwig Ott explains: "By dogma in the strict sense is understood a truth immediately (formally) revealed by God which has been proposed by the Teaching Authority of the Church to be believed as such."[322]

Indefectibility

Indefectibility means that Christ will be with His Church for all time and that it will last until the end of the world. "I am with you all days, even unto the consummation of the world."[323]

Heretics Pick and Choose

Although a cafeteria-style approach to religion, to pick and choose beliefs, has the appearance of religion, it lacks substance. Through the centuries rebellious religious leaders left the Catholic Church and formed religions of their own. Many of these still bear the names of their founders who either rejected beliefs or practices or developed new ones.

These leaders, who rejected the authority of the Catholic Church, set themselves up as experts in religious matters and became the ultimate religious authority. Some followed private interpretation of Scripture and likewise rejected Apostolic Tradition. Others questioned the consistent teachings of the Popes and the Fathers and Doctors of the Church.

Since manmade religions are subjective, they have inconsistencies and contradictions. The Catholic Church is the only religion in the world that has retained essentially the same beliefs and worship from its founding to the present day.

Heretics often exaggerate one doctrine of the Faith and deny others. They retain a semblance of Catholic teaching to more easily deceive followers. Heresy, a denial of one or more *de fide* doctrines of the Church, is based on pride and rebellion against God, His laws and His Church.

---

[320] *Pastor Aeternus*, c. 4. Pope Pius XII, *Munificentissimus Deus*, November 1, 1950.
[321] Denzinger 1792.
[322] *Fundamentals of Catholic Dogma*, p. 4.
[323] Matthew 28, 20.

All or Nothing

Catholic belief is a package deal—all or nothing. Consider the words of the Profession of Faith of the Council of Trent and the constitution *Nuper ad nos* of Pope Benedict XIV:

> Also all other things taught, defined and declared by the sacred canons and ecumenical Councils... I without hesitation accept and profess, and at the same time all things contrary thereto... I likewise condemn, reject and anathematize.[324]

> Likewise, all other things I accept and profess, which the Holy Roman Church accepts and professes, and I likewise condemn, reject and anathematize... all contrary things, both schisms and heresies, which have been condemned, rejected and anathematized by the same Church.[325]

A Catholic must believe all *de fide* dogmas of the Church. A practicing Catholic attends Mass on every Sunday and frequently receives the Sacraments of Penance and Holy Eucharist.

The Catholic Faith is a uniform whole whose doctrines and practices are closely linked to one another. Sacred Scripture, Apostolic Tradition, the writings of the Popes, General Councils, Fathers and Doctors of the Church,[326] and Saints convey the same message and do not contradict one other. If there seems to be a contradiction, it is due to misinterpretation.

Members of the Catholic Church

The *Baltimore Catechism* explains who are members and subjects of the Catholic Church:

> Baptized persons remain *members* of the Church as long as they are united to it by profession of the same faith and have not broken the bonds of communion with it. All validly baptized persons are *subjects* of the Church, even if they are not members. Hence they are obliged to obey the laws of the Church unless exempted. If, however, they are invincibly ignorant of the obligation to obey the laws of the Church, they do not sin by not obeying them.[327]

The Council of Trent clearly teaches that after the promulgation of the Gospel, the justification of a sinner through Jesus Christ—thereby restoring man to the state of grace

> ...cannot be effected except through the laver of regeneration or a desire for it, as it is written: Unless a man be born again of water and the Holy Spirit, he cannot enter into the kingdom of God (John 3, 5).[328]

The Mystical Body of Christ

Christ, the Son of God, established the New Law to replace the Old and called all to become members of His Church. The term *Mystical Body of Christ* has been used for centuries to describe the Catholic Church. St. Ambrose and St. Augustine speak of members of the Church being united to Christ and one another by the bond of charity. St. Augustine wrote: "The Catholic Church alone is the body of Christ..."[329] "His body is the Church, not this church or that church, but the Church throughout the whole world..."[330]

---

[324] Denzinger 1000, November 13, 1565, Pope Pius IV's papal bull *Injunctum Nobis*.

[325] Denzinger 1473, March 16, 1743.

[326] Fathers of the Church lived near the time of Our Lord. Doctors of the Church are eminent teachers of the Faith. These include Saints Albert the Great, Alphonsus Liguori, Ambrose, Anselm, Anthony of Padua, Athanasius, Augustine of Hippo Basil the Great, Venerable Bede, Bernard of Clairvaux, Bonaventure, Caesarius of Arles, Clement of Rome, Cyril of Alexandria, Cyril of Jerusalem, Dionysius, Ephrem, Epiphanius, Francis de Sales, Gregory Nazianzen, Gregory of Nyssa, Hilary of Poitiers, Pope St. Gregory the Great, Ignatius of Antioch, Irenaeus, Isidore of Seville, Jerome, John Chrysostom, John Damascene, John of the Cross, Justin the Martyr, Leander of Seville, Pope St. Leo the Great, Peter Canisius, Peter Chrysologus, Polycarp, Peter Damian, Robert Bellarmine, Thomas Aquinas, and Vincent of Lerins.

[327] p. 186, question 317 (a) and (b).

[328] Session VI, Canon 4, Denzinger 796. [sine lavacro regenerationis aut eius voto].

[329] *Letter 185*, section 50.

[330] *Enarrationes in Psalmos* LVI, I.

St. John Chrysostom called the Holy Eucharist the "Mystical Body."[331] St. Albert the Great used the words to describe the Catholic Church whose members receive the Body of Christ in the Holy Eucharist.

St. Paul explains the bond that exists between members of the Mystical Body of Christ:

> ...with all humility and meekness, with patience, bearing with one another in love, careful to preserve the unity of the Spirit in the bond of peace: one body and one Spirit, even as you were called in one hope of your calling; one Lord, one faith, one Baptism, one God and Father of all, who is above all, and throughout all, and in us all.[332]

The Vatican Council (1869-1870) *Dogmatic Constitution on the Church of Christ* states that the true Church is not a loosely knit institution.

> We declare that it has been so plainly determined in its founding that any societies whatsoever that are separated from the unity of faith or from communion with this body cannot in any way be said to be a part or a member of it.

> And it cannot be said to be diffused and distributed among the various Christian denominations; but it is an integrated unit, entirely coherent; and, in its conspicuous unity, it shows itself an undivided and indivisible body, which is the true Mystical Body of Christ.

Pope Pius XII wrote that through His Death on the Cross, Christ "left to His Church the immense treasury of the Redemption."[333] Christ distributes those graces to souls through the Catholic Church by means of the Mass and Sacraments whereby the members of the Church are sanctified and more closely united to Our Lord.

The Holy Ghost—the Soul of the Church

Pope Leo XIII wrote in the encyclical *Divinum Illud Munus:* "Let it suffice to say that as Christ is the Head of the Church, so is the Holy Ghost her soul."[334] St. Augustine says: "What the soul is in our body that is the Holy Ghost in Christ's Body the Church."[335] The Holy Ghost infallibly preserves Christ's teachings that have been passed from generation to generation and sanctifies the members of the Catholic Church through the graces it offers.

The Holy Ghost preserves the Church from teaching error and leading souls astray. Since God is immutable and all Three Persons of the Blessed Trinity share the same Divine Nature, it is impossible for the Holy Ghost to change the doctrine and worship established by Jesus Christ.

The overshadowing of the Holy Ghost over the Catholic Church is clearly manifested through the centuries by wondrous uniformity in doctrine as Christ's teachings are consistently taught and explained by Popes, General Councils, the Fathers and Doctors of the Church, and Saints. All writings seem to have emanated from the same pen. St. Vincent of Lerins said:

> Again in the Catholic Church itself, very great care is to be taken that we hold that which has been believed everywhere, always and by all [Catholic] men.[336]

---

[331] *Homily on the Resurrection of the Dead,* n. 8, Gaume edition, Paris 1834, p. 56 C.
[332] Ephesians 4, 2-6.
[333] *Mystici Corporis Christi,* 46, June 29, 1943.
[334] May 9, 1897.
[335] Serm. 187, *De Temp.*
[336] Rev. Vigilius Krull, CPPS, *Christian Denominations,* p. 43.

Redemption

Our Lord redeemed the human race and opened the Gates of Heaven by His Passion and Death on the Cross. "For God so loved the world that He gave His Only-Begotten Son, that those who believe in Him may not perish, but may have life everlasting."[337]

Jesus repaired for original sin and the sins of all, however each person is still responsible to work out his own salvation in fear and trembling.[338] Therefore, one must refrain from judging.

Christ emphatically said: "Do not judge, that you may not be judged. For with what judgment you judge, you shall be judged..."[339]

"For what a man sows, that he will also reap."[340] God expects everyone to live a virtuous life, die in the state of grace and be an inspiration to all.

Although Jesus died to repair for the sins of all, not all are saved. "...for this is My Blood of the new covenant, which is being shed [efficaciously] for many unto the forgiveness of sin."[341]

Extreme Views of Salvation Common Today

Many today erroneously believe they are automatically saved. Some think they are saved merely by accepting Jesus as their personal Savior. Others believe that because they are baptized, they can do whatever they want. None of these are correct.

Other attacks against the justice and mercy of God and free will of God and humans include:

Universal Salvation whereby all are saved even if they don't do what God commands[342] [343]

No one is saved unless they have received Baptism of water[344]

God predestines people to be saved or damned[345]

Justification

St. Thomas Aquinas wrote of the necessity of being incorporated into Jesus Christ since "...there is no other name under Heaven given men by which we must be saved."[346] The matter is elucidated by Canon Smith in his book *The Teaching of the Catholic Church Volume II:*

> Treating the question whether a man can be saved without Baptism, St. Thomas allows that where actual Baptism is absent due to accidental circumstances, the desire proceeding from 'faith working through charity' will in God's providence inwardly sanctify him. But where you have absence of actual Baptism and a culpable absence of the desire for Baptism, 'those who are not baptized under such conditions cannot be saved, because neither sacramentally nor mentally are they incorporated in Christ, through whom alone comes salvation.'[347]

---

[337] John 3, 16.
[338] Philippians 2, 12.
[339] Matthew 7, 1.
[340] Galatians 6, 8.
[341] Matthew 26, 28.
[342] Taught by Karl Rahner, (1904-1984) a heretical theologian at Vatican II.
[343] Pope Gregory XVI condemned religious indifferentism and the proposition "...that eternal salvation of the soul can be acquired by any profession of faith whatsoever..." in the encyclical *Mirari vos* of August 15, 1832.
[344] Taught by Fr. Leonard Feeney (1897-1978) and by others today. Pope Pius XII excommunicated Fr. Feeney on Feb. 12, 1953.
[345] Taught by heretic John Calvin (1509-1564).
[346] Acts of the Apostles 4, 12.
[347] p. 675. Romans 4, 11. III Q. 68, art. 2.

Pope Pius XII condemned the concept of universal salvation repeatedly.

> Some reduce to a meaningless formula the necessity of belonging to the True Church in order to gain eternal salvation.[348]

> Actually only those are to be included as members of the Church who have been baptized and profess the true faith, and who have not been so unfortunate as to separate themselves from the unity of the Body, or been excluded by legitimate authority for grave faults committed.[349]

The pope in the same encyclical explains the need for those outside the Catholic Church to join:

> We invite them all, each and everyone, to yield their free consent to the inner stirrings of God's grace and strive to extricate themselves from a state in which they cannot secure their own eternal salvation; for, though they may be related to the Mystical Body of the Redeemer by some unconscious yearning and desire, yet they are deprived of those many great and heavenly gifts and aids which can be enjoyed only in the Catholic Church.

> Let them enter Catholic unity, therefore, and join with us in the one organism of the Body of Jesus Christ, hasten together to the one Head in the fellowship of most glorious love. We cease not to pray for them to the Spirit of love and truth, and with open arms we await them, not as strangers but as those who are coming to their own Father's house.[350]

Baptism of Desire and Baptism of Blood

Many Catholics first learned about Baptism of desire and Baptism of blood from their lessons in the *Baltimore Catechism*. Dr. Ludwig Ott concisely summarizes[351] the matter:

> In case of emergency Baptism by water can be replaced by Baptism of desire or Baptism of blood.

> **a) Baptism of desire** *(Baptismus flaminis sive Spiritus Sancti)*

> Baptism of desire is the explicit or implicit desire for sacramental Baptism *(votum baptismi)* associated with perfect contrition (contrition based on charity).

> ...According to the teaching of Holy Writ [Sacred Scripture] perfect love possesses justifying power. 'Many sins are forgiven her because she hath loved much.'[352] 'He that loveth Me shall be loved of My Father: and I will love Him and will manifest Myself to him.'[353] 'This day thou shalt be with me in Paradise.'[354]

> Baptism of desire works *ex opere operantis* [*from the efforts of the person*]. It bestows sanctifying grace, which remits original sin and all actual sins, and the eternal punishment for sin. ...

> **b) Baptism of blood** *(Baptismus sanguinis)*

> Baptism of blood signifies martyrdom of an unbaptized person, that is, the patient [person suffering] of a violent death or an assault which of its nature leads to death, by reason of one's confession of the Christian [Catholic] faith, or one's practice of Christian virtue.

> ...From the beginning the Fathers regarded martyrdom as a substitute for Baptism. ...Blood-Baptism operates not merely *ex opere operantis*... but since it is an objective confession of Faith it operates also quasi *ex opere operato* [*through the action having been accomplished*]. It confers the grace of justification, and when proper dispositions are present, also the remission of all venial sins and temporal punishment.[355]

---

[348] *Humani Generis*, Paragraphs 45 and 42.
[349] *Mystici Corporis Christi*, 22.
[350] *Mystici Corporis Christi*, 103.
[351] A Teaching proximate to the Faith *(Sententia fidei proxima)* is a doctrine, which is regarded by theologians as a truth of Revelation, but which has not yet been finally promulgated as such by the Church. *Fundamentals of Catholic Dogma*, p. 9.
[352] Luke 7, 47.
[353] John 14, 21.
[354] Luke 23, 43.
[355] Ott, p. 356-357.

The *Baltimore Catechism* teaches:

> Baptism of desire takes away all sin, original and actual, and the eternal punishment due to sin. It does not, however, imprint a character on the soul, nor does it necessarily take away all the temporal punishment due to actual sins.

> Baptism of blood does not imprint a character on the soul, nor does it give one the right to receive the other sacraments. It does, however, confer grace and take away sin, original and actual, and the punishment due to sin.[356]

Those who become members of the Catholic Church by Baptism of desire and Baptism of blood must necessarily have either an explicit or implicit desire to receive the Sacrament of Baptism and to do whatever else God commands. Therefore, the infallible doctrine of outside the Church there is no salvation applies to these individuals because they have been justified and thus die in the state of sanctifying grace as members of the Catholic Church.

Some today falsely claim these are erroneous teachings because they condone a type of universal salvation. This is not the case. Baptism of desire and Baptism of blood are frequently found in the writings of the Fathers and Doctors of the Church, the Popes and General Councils of the Church, including the Council of Trent.

The Catholic Church works untiringly for the salvation of immortal souls and the conversion of sinners. Catechumens study the Faith as they prepare to receive the Sacrament of Baptism. Others learn about Catholic beliefs through priests, Religious Sisters, Catholic friends, missionaries, or even the media.

Baptism of desire and Baptism of blood are not sacraments, yet, through the will of Christ, they effect justification just as Baptism of water does. They do not leave an indelible mark on the soul. Our Lord chose Baptism by water as the means whereby individuals become members of His Church. Baptism of desire and Baptism of blood are the exception to the rule because they act as substitutes when Baptism of water cannot be received.

God can do as He pleases. Even though a ticket is the normal means of entrance into a sporting event, some people get sideline passes. Both have the same effect. One is the norm, the other the exception. Numerous Fathers of the Church explain.

> St. Bernard invokes the authority of SS. Ambrose and Augustine in support of his teaching that a man may be saved by the Baptism of desire if death or some other insuperable obstacle prevents him from receiving Baptism of water.[357]

St. Augustine wrote:

> Nor do I hesitate to put a Catholic catechumen burning with divine love before a baptized heretic... For the centurion Cornelius, not yet baptized, is better than Simon [the Magician] baptized. For he was filled with the Holy Ghost before Baptism, but the other, after Baptism was filled with the evil spirit.[358]

> For whatever unbaptized persons die confessing Christ, this confession is of the same efficacy for the remission of sins as if they were washed in the sacred font of Baptism.

---

[356] pp. 188-189.
[357] *Ep. 77 ad Hug Vict.*, n. 8: *"Ab his duabus columnis difficile avellor; cum his, inquam, aut sapere me fateor, credens et ipse sola fide* [i.e. formata] *posse hominem salvari cum desiderio percipiendi sacramentum, si tamen pio implendi desiderio mors anticipans seu alia quaecumque vis imvincibilis obviaverit."* (Migne, *Patr. Lat.*, CLXXXII, 1036).
[358] *The City of God*, Bk. 4, Ch. 21.

For He who said, 'Except a man be born of water and of the Spirit, he cannot enter into the kingdom of God' (John 3, 5), made an exception in their favor, in that other sentence where He no less absolutely said, 'Whosoever shall confess Me before men, I will confess also before My Father Who is in Heaven' (Matthew 10, 32).[359]

I find that not only martyrdom for the sake of Christ may supply what was wanting of Baptism, but also faith and conversion of heart, if recourse can not be had to the celebration of the mystery of Baptism for want of time.[360]

St. Cyprian is even more emphatic:

Some, as if by human reasoning they were able to make void the truth of the Gospel declaration, object to us in the case of catechumens; asking if any one of these, before he is baptized in the Church, should be apprehended and slain on confession of the name [of Jesus], whether he would lose the hope of salvation and the reward of confession, because he had not previously been born again of water?

Let men of this kind, who are aiders and favorers of heretics, know therefore, first, that those catechumens hold the sound faith and truth of the Church, and advance from the divine camp to do battle with the devil, with a full and sincere acknowledgement of God the Father, and of Christ, and of the Holy Ghost; then, that they certainly are not deprived of the Sacrament of Baptism who are baptized with the most glorious and greatest baptism of blood, concerning which the Lord also said, that He had a 'another baptism to be baptized with' (Luke 12, 50).

But the same Lord declares in the Gospel, that those who are baptized in their own blood, and sanctified by suffering, are perfected, and obtain the grace of the divine promise, when He speaks to the thief believing and confessing in His very Passion, and promises that he should be with Himself in Paradise.[361]

Msgr. Pohle gives additional proofs from Scripture:

The supernatural efficacy of martyrdom may be deduced from our Lord's declaration in Matthew...'He that findeth his life, shall lose it; and he that shall lose his life for Me shall find it.'[362]

St. Bonaventure writes about martyrdom for the Catholic Faith:

...in the Baptism of blood there is an ampler and a fuller imitation and profession of the Passion of Christ than in the Baptism of water... In the Baptism of water death is signified; in the Baptism of blood it is incurred.[363]

Catechumens Receive Catholic Burial

Regarding Catholic burial, Canon 1239 (2) clearly states:

Catechumens [unbaptized individuals taking instructions in the Faith] who, through no fault of their own, die without having received Baptism are to be treated as baptized.[364]

---

[359] *The City of God,* Bk. 13, Ch. 7.

[360] *De Baptismo contra Donat.,* IV, 22: *"Invenio, non tantum passionem pro Christo id quod ex baptismo deerat posse supplere, sed etiam fidem conversionemque cordis, si forte ad celebrandum mysterium in angustiis temporum succurri non potest."*

[361] *Letters,* No. 73: 22.

[362] Matthew 10, 39, Cfr. Matthew 16, 25; Luke 9, 24; 17, 33.

[363] *Comment. in Sent.,* IV, dist 4, p. 2, art. I, qu. 2, ad 2: *"Ratio autem quare efficiam habet maiorem est, quoniam in baptismo sanguinis amplior et plenior est imitatio et professio passionis Christi quam in baptismo aquae mors significatur, hic autem suscipitur."* For a fuller treatment of this topic cfr. Gihr, *Die hl. Sakramente der kath. Kirche,* Vol. I, 2nd ed., pp. 271 sqq.

[364] Catechumeni qui nulla sua culpa sine baptismo moriantur, baptismatis accensendi sunt.

Nulla Salus Extra Ecclesiam

The *Letter of the Holy Office to Cardinal Cushing* of August 8, 1949 says:

> The infallible dictum which teaches us that outside the Church there is no salvation, is among the truths the Church has always taught and always will teach.

> But this dogma is to be understood as the Church itself understands it. For our Savior did not leave it to private judgment to explain what is contained in the Deposit of Faith, but to the doctrinal authority of the Church.[365]

> ...Therefore, no one who knows that the Church has been divinely established by Christ, and nevertheless, refuses to be a subject of the Church or refuses to obey the Roman Pontiff, the vicar of Christ on earth, will be saved.

Canon George Smith writes:

> Evidently, if the Church is the Mystical Body of Christ, then to be outside the Mystical Body is to be outside the Church, and since there is no salvation outside the Mystical Body, there is no salvation outside the Church.[366]

Chapter One of the Fourth Lateran Council (1215) document on the Catholic Faith says: "One indeed is the universal Church of the faithful, outside which no one at all is saved..."[367] The Profession of Faith of the Council of Trent teaches: "This true Catholic faith, outside of which no one can be saved..."[368]

Pope Eugene IV wrote the papal bull *Cantate Domino*[369] during the Council of Florence that attempted to return schismatic churches of the East to the Catholic Church. Unfortunately, large numbers of orthodox leaders and their people remained in bad faith. Many of these were killed when their countries were overtaken by Muslim armies. At the same time, other orthodox leaders and their formerly schismatic churches rejoined the Catholic Faith. The document conveys both ideas.

> The Most Holy Roman Church, founded by the voice of our Lord and Savior... firmly believes, professes, and proclaims that those not living within the Catholic Church... cannot become participants in eternal life, ...unless before the end of life the same have been added to the flock; ...and that no one, whatever almsgivings he has practiced, even if he has shed blood for the name of Christ [professing a non-Catholic religion], can be saved, unless he has remained in the bosom and unity of the Catholic Church.[370]

Invincible Ignorance

Pope Pius IX condemned the erroneous concept as contrary to Catholic teaching that "men living in error, and separated from the true faith and from Catholic unity, can attain eternal life."[371] The same pope describes invincible ignorance as something different in two encyclicals.

> For, it must be held by faith that outside the Apostolic Roman Church, no one can be saved; that this is the only ark of salvation; that he who shall not have entered therein will perish in the flood; but, on the other hand, it is necessary to hold for certain that those who labor in ignorance of the true religion, if this ignorance is invincible, are not stained by any guilt in this matter in

---

[365] See John Clarkson, SJ, *The Church Teaches*, p. 119.
[366] Canon George Smith, DD, PhD, *The Teaching of the Catholic Church Vol. II*, p. 677.
[367] Denzinger 430. St. Cyprian: "There is no salvation outside the Church," Ep. 73, To Iubaianus, n. 21 [Migne *Patrologiae Cursus completus. Series prima Latina*, Parisis, 1844 (tomus I), 3, 1123 B.]
[368] Denzinger 1000.
[369] February 4, 1441.
[370] Denzinger 703, 714. Cf. St. Fulgentius, *De fide*, ad Petrum c. 37 ff., n. 78 ff. [Migne].
[371] *Quanto conficiamur moerore*, August 10, 1863. Denzinger 1677, See *Syllabus of Errors*, no. 17, Denzinger 1717.

the eyes of God. Now, in truth, who would arrogate so much to himself as to mark the limits of such an ignorance, because of the nature and variety of peoples, regions, innate dispositions, and of so many other things?[372]

There are, of course, those who are struggling with invincible ignorance about our most holy religion. Sincerely observing the natural law and its precepts inscribed by God on all hearts and ready to obey God, they live honest lives and are able to attain eternal life by the efficacious virtue of divine light and grace. Because God knows, searches and clearly understands the minds, hearts, thoughts, and nature of all, His supreme kindness and clemency do not permit anyone at all who is not guilty of deliberate sin to suffer eternal punishments.

Also well known is the Catholic teaching that no one can be saved outside the Catholic Church. Eternal salvation cannot be obtained by those who oppose the authority and statements of the same Church and are stubbornly separated from the unity of the Church...[373]

Pope Innocent III wrote a letter[374] to Berthold, Bishop of Metz on August 28, 1206 about a Jewish man who lived among non-Catholics who attempted to baptize himself. The pope said that he needed to be baptized by another if he was still alive.

If, however, such a one had died immediately, he would have rushed to his heavenly home without delay because of the faith of the sacrament, although not because of the sacrament of faith [because he tried invalidly to confer Baptism on himself].[375]

Perfect Contrition

St. Alphonsus Ligouri in his *Sermons* wrote: "God cannot turn away His face from those who cast themselves at His feet with a humble and contrite heart. ...Oh! with what tenderness does God embrace a sinner that returns to Him!" Think of St. Mary Magdalen.

Eminent Doctor of the Church, St. Robert Bellarmine said: "Repentance destroys all sin."[376] Perfect contrition is often a clear manifestation of one's love for God. St. John Climacus taught:

Total [Perfect] Contrition is necessary for everyone, but particularly for those who have come to the King to obtain forgiveness of their sins.[377]

Supernatural Faith and Charity

The *Letter of the Holy Office*[378] of August 8, 1949 explaining Baptism of desire and blood said:

But it must not be thought that any kind of desire of entering the Church suffices that one may be saved. It is necessary that the desire by which one is related to the Church be animated by perfect charity. Nor can an implicit desire produce its effect, without supernatural faith. ...

The Council of Trent[379] declares:

Faith is the beginning of man's salvation, the foundation and root of all justification, without which it is impossible to please God and attain to the fellowship of His children.[380]

---

[372] *Singulari quadem,* December 9, 1854, Denzinger 1647.
[373] *Quanto conficiamur moerore,* August 10, 1863. Par. 6-7. Similar to *Unam Sanctam* of Pope Boniface VIII, Denzinger 468-469.
[374] *Debitum Pastoralis Officii.*
[375] Denzinger 413.
[376] *The Mind's Ascent to God by the Ladder of Created Things.*
[377] *The Ladder of Divine Ascent.*
[378] Prot. N. 122/49.
[379] Session VI, chap. 8.
[380] Denzinger 801. See Hebrews 11, 6.

Fr. Francis Connell, CSSR wrote:

> The *virtue* or *habit* of faith is necessary for salvation by absolute necessity of means. For no one
> can be saved unless he leaves this world in the state of sanctifying grace; and one who leaves this
> world in sanctifying grace always possesses the virtue of faith.[381]

St. Francis de Sales described the link between faith and charity when he wrote:

> When charity is united and joined to faith, it vivifies it. ...Just as the soul cannot remain in the
> body without producing vital actions, so charity cannot be united to our faith without performing
> works conforming to it.[382]

Obedience to God and His laws, and supernatural faith and charity are necessary for salvation.
"So there abide faith, hope and charity, these three; but the greatest of these is charity." [383]

Popes Remind All to Leave Final Judgment Up to God

Since Jesus Christ died on the Cross in order to redeem the human race, He will judge each
individual at the Particular Judgment at death, and all mankind, at the General Judgment.

God Who sees everything judges justly and impartially. Mercy and justice are perfectly
balanced in Him as described in the Second Book of Machabees (1, 24-25).

> ...Lord God, Creator of all things, dreadful and strong, just and merciful, Who alone art the Good
> King, Who alone art gracious, Who alone art just and almighty and eternal...

In the allocution *Singulari quadem* of December 9, 1854, Pope Pius IX stated:

> Far be it from Us, Venerable Brethren, to presume on the limits of the divine mercy which is
> infinite; far from Us, to wish to scrutinize the hidden counsel and 'judgments of God' which are 'a
> great deep' and cannot be penetrated by human thought.

For individuals to authoritatively say who is saved and who is not is rash and foolhardy. In his
encyclical *Mirari vos* Pope Gregory XVI wrote:

> It is characteristic of the proud, or rather of the foolish man to test the mysteries of faith 'which
> surpasseth all understanding' [Phil. 4, 7] by human standards, and to entrust them to the
> reasoning of our mind, which by reason of the condition of our human nature is weak and
> infirm.[384]

Those who sit in judgment of others resemble the Pharisee who praised himself while
lamenting the terrible sins of the repentant publican as related in Luke 18, 9-14.

> I tell you, this man [the repentant publican] went back to his home justified rather than the
> other; for everyone who exalts himself shall be humbled, and he who humbles himself shall be
> exalted.

Jesus Who forgave St. Dismas and praised the faith of the centurion at Capharnaum whose son
He cured[385] will alone be the Final Judge and determine who is saved and who is eternally lost.

Judge Not That You May not be Judged

Mother Elizabeth Seton in her *Collected Works* lamented how frequently people err in
judgment because they are unaware of the motives of others. Only God sees the heart. In his
Letter to the Soldiers of Coroticus, St. Patrick simply stated: "God alone will judge."

---

[381] *Outlines in Moral Theology,* p. 71.
[382] *Oeuvres.*
[383] 1 Corinthinians 13, 13.
[384] Denzinger 1616.
[385] Matthew 8, 10-11.

Chapter Thirty-Six
The Deposit of Faith

The *Deposit of Faith* contains the chief truths of the Catholic Church that all Catholics are bound to believe. It consists of *Sacred Scripture* and *Apostolic Tradition*.

Sacred Scripture is the revealed word of God. It begins with the five books written by Moses called the Pentateuch and ends with the Apocalypse of St. John the Evangelist (+100 AD). Divine Revelation ceased after the death of the Apostle, St. John.

Sacred Scripture

The Catholic Bible contains 45 Old Testament books and 27 New Testament books. *Bible* is a Greek word for *the books* or *the book*. St. Jerome referred to it as the Divine Library.

Although various authors wrote the books of the Bible, they were inspired on what to write. Therefore, God is the author of the Bible. St. Thomas Aquinas said, "the Holy Ghost is the principal Author of Scripture." St. Augustine referred to the Bible as God's handwriting and St. Bonaventure called it "the voice of God."[386]

Ptolemy II (285-247 BC) desired a Greek version of the Old Testament and employed 70 scholars from Jerusalem to complete the task in Alexandria, Egypt. The work that began around 300 BC was completed in 130 BC. The *Septuagint* was used by Christ and His Apostles when quoting Old Testament texts, and by the Early Church.

Once the Roman Persecutions ended, scriptural manuscripts were gathered from around the world. Many were preserved in Rome, Antioch, Alexandria, and other major Christian centers. A number of submitted writings were considered Apocryphal—unauthentic, non-scriptural texts. Some were even composed by heretics to promote false beliefs.

Pope St. Damasus I commissioned St. Jerome to write the Latin *Vulgate*, the official Bible of the Catholic Church. The work began in 383 and was completed in 405 AD.

There are 72 canonical books in the Catholic Bible. These books were determined to be authentic and divinely inspired by the Council of Laodicea in 367, the Council of Carthage, where it was formally approved by Pope St. Damasus I in 397 AD and by the Council of Trent in 1546. The world owes the preservation of the New Testament to the Catholic Church.

The oldest existing codices (copies) of the Bible written on parchment or papyrus include:

Name	Year of Composition	Present Location	
Codex Vaticanus	(early fourth century)	Vatican Library	(Vatican City)
Codex Sinaiticus	(fourth century)	St. Catherine Monastery	(Mt. Sinai)
Codex Alexandrinus	(fifth century)	Alexandria / Constantinople	(Istanbul)
Codex Ephraemi[387]	(fifth century)	Bibliothèque Nationale de France	(Paris)

---

[386] In Hexam., 12.

[387] A palimpsest—in the twelfth century scribes wrote over the original text with writings of St. Ephrem.

Popular Approved English Translations

Douay-Rheims version (1609-1610)

Bishop Challoner revision (1749-1752)

Confraternity of Christian Doctrine revision (1941)

Biblical Chapter and Verse

Catholics made the chapter and verse divisions in the Bible. Archbishop of Canterbury Stephen Langton divided the Bible into chapters in the 1200s, Dominican Santes Pagnino designated verses for the Old Testament in the 1500s and Paris printer Robert Stephen gave verse notations to the New Testament in the 1600s.

Books Missing from Protestant Bibles

Even though many Protestant sects today teach that faith is to be based on Scripture Only (*Sola Scriptura*) they use a defective bible. Besides at times being purposely mistranslated,[388] Protestant bibles are missing the books of Tobias, Judith, Wisdom, Ecclesiasticus, Baruch, and First and Second Machabees. They also omit chapter 10, verse 4 and chapter 16, verse 24 from the Book of Esther and chapter 3, verses 24-90 and chapters 13 and 14 from Daniel. The deleted books are found in the Septuagint (Alexandrian version) that Jesus and the Apostles used, but absent from the Palestinian version that Protestant scholars adopted.

Apostolic Tradition

Apostolic Tradition is comprised of the doctrinal teachings and liturgical practices that have been handed down from Christ through the Apostles. *Tradition* is derived from a Latin word meaning *handed down*. It is often reflected in the writings of the early Fathers of the Church who lived at the time of the Apostles or shortly thereafter.

St. Paul said, "So then, brethren, stand firm, and hold the tradition that you have learned, whether by word or by letter of ours."[389] The 1941 Confraternity of Christian Doctrine translation of the New Testament has a footnote on this verse that says these teachings are both oral and written and notes that "Hence not all apostolic teaching was written in the books of the New Testament."

The last words of St. John's Gospel reflect that the Evangelists could not possibly record all that Jesus did or taught during His Public Life and the 40 days after the Resurrection.

> There are, however, many other things that Jesus did; but if every one of these should be written, not even the world itself, I think, could hold the books that would have to be written...

Sacred Scripture and Apostolic Tradition are complimentary and support one another. They are God's Revelation—the Deposit of the Faith.

St. Peter, the first pope, demonstrates the absolute need for a teaching Church when he wrote:

> In these epistles there are certain things difficult to understand, which the unlearned and the unstable distort, just as they do the rest of the Scriptures also, to their own destruction.[390]

---

[388] See Matthew 6, 7, 1 Corinthians 11, 27, Luke 1, 28 and Luke 2, 14 among others.
[389] 2 Thessolonians, 2, 14. Douay Rheims translation.
[390] 2 Peter 3, 16.

Chapter Thirty-Seven

The Four Marks of the Catholic Church

Since there are so many different religions in the world, how can someone distinguish the one, true church from man-made religions? Four marks are shared by only one church—the Catholic Church founded by Jesus Christ. St. Cyril of Jerusalem describes the Catholic Church as the "Holy Church, the Mother of us all, who is the Bride of Our Lord Jesus Christ, the only-begotten Son of God."[391]

One (Unity) The Catholic Faith is one in doctrine, worship and authority. *It has the same essential beliefs, Mass and sacraments all over the world.* St. Irenaeus wrote:

> Just as the sun is one and the same in the whole world, so the message of truth penetrates everywhere and enlightens all men, who wish to come to the knowledge of the truth.[392]

Holy (Holiness) Christ, Who is all-holy, founded the Catholic Church. *It offers the means of sanctification to make one holy—the Holy Sacrifice of the Mass and the Seven Sacraments.*

The Catholic Church produces saintly men, women and children whom St. Peter described as "... a chosen generation, a holy people."[393] Pope Pius XII wrote:

> ...in the Sacraments with which she begets and nourishes her children; in the faith which she preserves ever inviolate; in the holy laws she imposes on all and in the evangelical counsels by which she admonishes; and, finally, in the heavenly gifts and miraculous powers by which out of her inexhaustible fecundity she begets a countless host of martyrs, virgins and confessors.[394]

Catholic (Catholicity) The Church Christ founded is catholic—universal. *All Catholics have the same beliefs and worship and the same Faith is found all over the world.* St. Cyril wrote: "She is called Catholic since she alone has the privilege of being known in the whole world, and of having subjects in all parts of the world."[395]

St. Ignatius of Antioch is claimed to be the first person to address the Church with title catholic. "Where Jesus Christ is, there is the Catholic Church."[396] The word "catholic" is found in the Nicene-Constantinopolitan Creed (381 AD). St. Thomas Aquinas teaches that the catholicity of the Church is based on its extension over the entire world, on the universality of classes represented and on the fact that the Church will last until the end of time.[397]

Apostolic (Apostolicity) *The Catholic Church was founded by Christ on the 12 Apostles. Their successors are the Catholic bishops.* This is called *Apostolic Succession.* Dr. Ludwig Ott says: "The apostolic character of Church most clearly appears in the unbroken succession of the bishops from the Apostles."[398] Bishops have the fullness of the priesthood and ordain priests who serve parishes throughout the world. This allows the Church to fulfill Christ's mission for all time to "Go into the whole world and preach the gospel to every creature." (Mark 16, 15).

---

[391] Cat. 18, 26.
[392] Adv. haer. I 10, 2; Cf. V 20, 1.
[393] 1 Peter 2, 9.
[394] *Mystici Corporis Christi,* June 29, 1943.
[395] *Exposition of Christian Doctrine: Part I Dogma,* p. 452.
[396] Smyrn. 8, 2.
[397] Expos. symb. a. 9. See Dr. Ludwig Ott, *Fundamentals of Catholic Dogma,* p. 308.
[398] *Fundamentals of Catholic Dogma,* p. 308.

Religion

Many people today don't understand religion and believe it is a manmade invention used to control people. Although the word *religion* is derived from a Latin word that means *to bind*, the Catholic Faith lovingly unites human beings to God, their Creator. Since Jesus Christ the Son of God founded the Catholic Church, it is God-made, not of human origin.

If all religions are the same or lead to the same place as ecumenists contend, Jesus Christ should have never come to earth. Our Lord spent three years teaching definitive doctrines to the Apostles and His followers, instituted the Mass and sacraments, established a hierarchy, and promised that *His* Church would last until the end of time.

A Visible Church

Since God is the ultimate source of truth and goodness, His Church, the Catholic Church portrays these characteristics. It is a visible church with a divine appointed hierarchy.

Prayer is the way people talk and communicate with God. It is a loving conversation between the creature and the Creator. The Holy Sacrifice of the Mass and Seven Sacraments draw down graces from God needed to overcome sin and temptation and practice virtue. The teachings of the Church show the path to Heaven. God's laws and those of the Church preserve order and in society and in the lives of individuals. Their observance is the ultimate proof of ones' love for Almighty God.

Manmade Churches

Humans are fallible and prone to extremes. Organized religion is necessary since disorganized religion becomes a free-for-all where leaders impose *their* opinions on others. Without proper, unbiased, objective guidance people easily become deluded and end up getting lost—like those who wander through a strange forest without a compass or GPS.[399]

---

[399] Global Postitioning System.

Chapter Thirty-Eight

The Laws of Fast and Abstinence

Our Lord said, "Unless you do penance you shall all likewise perish." (Luke 13, 3) Although penance is sacrificial and difficult and no one likes to perform it, when done in moderation and for a proper reason, penances such as fasting, and abstinence from meat, honor God, strengthen the will, help tame human nature, and assist one to gain mastery over the passions. Fasting teaches humility and has been in use since the earliest ages of the Church.

The followers of St. John the Baptist asked Jesus why His Apostles didn't fast. Jesus replied, "Can the wedding guests mourn as long as the bridegroom is with them? But the days will come when the bridegroom shall be taken away from them, and then they will fast."[400]

Fasting has been practiced since time immemorial. Isaias, Moses, Elias, Ezechiel, and other holy men were known for their fasting. When Jonas warned the Assyrians to repent, "...the men of Ninive believed in God: and they proclaimed a fast, and put on sackcloth from the greatest to the least." (Jonas 3, 5) God spared their city as a result.

The Catholic Church instituted the 40 days of fasting (excluding Sundays) during Lent from Ash Wednesday to Holy Saturday in memory of Our Lord's 40 day fast in the desert. Jesus showed how powerful fasting is when He said that certain devils could not be expelled except through prayer and fasting.

Church Laws of Fasting for the United States

1. The law of fast applies to all Catholics 21-59 years of age.

2. Fast days include the weekdays during Lent, Holy Saturday, Ember Days, and the Vigils of Pentecost, the Immaculate Conception & Christmas.

3. Only one full meal is allowed on a day of fast. A person may have two other meatless meals to maintain one's strength. Combined, these should be less than the main meal.

4. Meat may be eaten at the main meal on a day of fast except on Fridays, Ash Wednesday, Holy Saturday, and the Vigils of the Immaculate Conception & Christmas.

5. Although those fasting can't eat between meals, they may drink milk, coffee and juices, and the like.

6. When health or the ability to work would be seriously affected, the law does not oblige. One who is not obliged to fast may eat meat as often as he wills on days when fasting alone is prescribed. In doubt concerning either fasting or abstinence, one should consult his confessor or pastor.[401] Lent ceases at Midnight on Holy Saturday according to the regulations of the Restored Holy Week.[402]

---

[400] Matthew 9, 15.
[401] Rev. Heribert Jone, OFM, Cap. JCD, *Moral Theology,* p. 263.
[402] Jone, 265.

Those dispensed from the laws of fast include those who are ill, individuals who are under a doctor's care such as diabetics, pregnant and nursing mothers, and those who do heavy work. "Professors, teachers, students, preachers, confessors, physicians, judges, lawyers, etc. are excused if fasting would hinder them in their work."[403]

Church Laws of Abstinence for the United States

1. All Catholics age seven and older are bound to observe the law of abstinence.

2. Complete abstinence is followed on all Fridays, Ash Wednesday, Holy Saturday, and the Vigils of the Immaculate Conception and Christmas. On days of complete abstinence one may not consume meat and soup or gravy made from meat.

3. Partial abstinence is followed on Ember Wednesdays and Saturdays and on the Vigil of Pentecost. On days of partial abstinence one may consume meat and soup or gravy that is made from meat only once daily, at the main meal.

4. There is no abstinence from meat on Holydays of Obligation that fall on a Friday.

5. American bishops gave a dispensation from meat when the Fourth of July falls on a Friday and also on the Friday after Thanksgiving.

6. "Catholics serving in the Armed Forces, while they are in actual service, and their families, too, when eating with them, are dispensed from abstinence except on Ash Wednesday, Good Friday, Holy Saturday (the entire day), and the Vigil of Christmas."[404]

Catholics do not eat meat on Fridays to remind themselves that Jesus died for the sins of the world on Good Friday.

It is a mortal sin to purposely eat meat on Friday unless it is a grave inconvenience to do so. One may use lard and gelatin on days of abstinence.

---

[403] Rev. Heribert Jone, OFM, Cap. JCD, *Moral Theology,* p. 265.
[404] Jone, 262.

Chapter Thirty-Nine

Indulgences

The concept of indulgences is based on mercy and justice. Good actions should be rewarded and evil ones punished. Restitution restores proper order and makes reparation for the offense committed. The criminal justice system used today in the United States punishes crime (sin), gives credit for time served and good behavior, and occasionally grants pardon and early parole. If society can pardon and credit good actions, why can't the Catholic Church?

The word indulgence comes from a Latin word *indulgére* which means *to be kind, to forgive, to be lenient towards*. The word also formerly meant *the forgiveness of a debt*. The practice of the Church granting indulgences goes back at least to the First Council of Nicaea (325 AD).

What are Indulgences?

Indulgences are granted for the recitation of ecclesiastically approved prayers (the Rosary, Stations of the Cross and prayers that have indulgences listed with the imprimatur of a specific pope or bishop[405] *or for the performance of good works* (visits to a church or cemetery, etc.). The *Raccolta* is the official book of the Catholic Church that contains indulgenced prayers and lists indulgenced good works.

Partial indulgences given for an indulgenced prayer or work refers to the equivalent value of days or years spent in public penance (100, 300 or 500 days) or (one, five or seven years), not to time spent in Purgatory.

Some of those who renounced the Catholic Faith or committed public scandal in the early ages of the Church were required to make reparation by means of *public penance*. This usually consisted of attending Mass up to the Offertory,[406] refraining from receiving Holy Communion for a number of years and fasting on bread and water. This custom is no longer in use.

A *plenary indulgence* removes all the temporal punishment due for the sins one has committed. This indulgence does not replace sacramental confession or receiving absolution from a priest.

Conditions Required to Gain an Indulgence

Three conditions necessary to gain a partial or plenary indulgence are to be in the state of grace, desire to receive the indulgence[407] and fulfill the required conditions.

The *usual conditions* to gain an indulgence are:

1) Sacramental Confession (within eight days before or after)

2) Reception of Holy Communion (on the vigil, day or within a week)

3) Our Father, Hail Mary and Glory Be prayed for the intention of the Roman Pontiff.[408]

---

[405] From the Latin: *let it be printed*. The words: "With ecclesiastical permission" are vague and insufficient.

[406] Called the Mass of the Catechumens.

[407] A habitual implicit intention, such as after receiving the Apostolic Blessing is sufficient. See *The Sacred Canons* Vol. II, John Abbo, STL, JCD and Jerome Hannan, AM, LLB, STD, JCD, pp. 51-52 footnote 5.

[408] See *AAS*, XXV, 446. The person seeking to gain an indulgence doesn't have to know what the intentions are (listed on the following page). The condition applies whether there is a reigning pope or an *interregnum* (time between the reign of popes).

The intentions of the Roman Pontiff are:

...the exaltation of the Church, the propagation of the faith, ending of heresy and schism, conversion of sinners, peace and harmony among Christian rulers and nations, and other blessings for the welfare of Christianity.[409]

4) To gain a *toties quoties* indulgence that requires a visit to a church or oratory, six sets of Our Fathers, Hail Marys and Glory Bes must be recited for the intention of the pope.[410]

Some indulgences are applicable only to the Faithful Departed such as the *toties quoties* indulgence on November 1 and 2.

Praying with Others

It is customary to vocalize part of public prayers when joining others in church for the Rosary and the Way of the Cross. The leader says the first part of the prayers, while the congregation answers. Families often have their children lead individual decades.

The same is done during the public recitation of the Divine Office when one person leads the psalms and the others answer. In order to gain indulgences from vocal prayers, it is necessary to move one's lips while praying.

It is important not to *race* through prayers to get them over or *echo* prayers—pray slower than others when reciting them in a group. Those who say prayers rapidly often don't reflect on what they are saying. Those who pray too slowly destroy unity when joining others.

Common prayer should honor God and edify others by being recited in a uniform speed—not too fast and not too slow. The psalms compare prayer to incense arising to God.

St. Louis de Montfort describes to benefit of praying with others.

Normally our minds are far more alert during public prayer than they are when we pray alone. When we pray in common, the prayer of each one belongs to us all and these make but one great prayer together, so that if one person is not praying well, someone else in the same gathering who prays better may make up for his deficiency. In this way, those who are strong uphold the weak, those who are fervent inspire the lukewarm... Someone who says his Rosary alone only gains the merit of one Rosary, but if he says it together with thirty other people he gains the merit of thirty Rosaries.[411]

Avarice Still Here Today

In the year 1513, the pope granted an indulgence for those contributing to the construction of St. Peter's Basilica. Although there were some abuses regarding indulgences during the sixteenth century, the practice of indulgences is not evil and the Catholic Church has never condoned the sale of indulgences.

The allure of money has lead to the downfall of many, including Judas, one of the Apostles. The 25-year-old Archbishop Albrecht of Mainz saw the indulgence as an opportunity to pocket money destined for the construction of St. Peter's to help pay off his own debts.[412] This parallels those who embezzle money destined for charitable organizations today.

---

[409] Rev. Stanislaus Woywod, OFM, LLB, *A Practical Commentary on the Code of Canon Law*, p. 538.
[410] See *Acta XXII*, July 5, 1930.
[411] *The Secret of the Rosary*, pp. 96-97.
[412] See Frs. Francisco and Dominic Radecki, CMRI *Tumultuous Times*, pp. 187-188.

Chapter Forty

Life, Death, Judgment, Heaven, Hell

God expects one's best, like people expect excellence from cooks and waiters in a restaurant, from a pilot and flight attendant on a plane, from doctors and medical personnel in a hospital, and athletes on the field. Society doesn't reward mediocrity and neither can God.

Life

Life has one ultimate goal: for individuals to merit the unending happiness of Heaven. Everything else is insignificant. If this goal is not reached, one's life is a failure. Our Lord spoke of this when He said, "For what does it profit a man, if he gain the whole world, but suffer the loss of his own soul? Or what will a man give in exchange for his soul?"[413]

How can one merit an eternity of happiness with God if that person doesn't know Him or has rarely spoken with Him in prayer? God doesn't reward pride and selfishness. Actions committed here and now have eternal ramifications. Life passes in a flash. A person is here one day and gone the next. Once eternity begins, it has no end.

Although life is a series of trials, tests and temptations, it is also a means of meriting graces by patiently enduring temporal sufferings. Remain in the state of grace in order to avoid dying in mortal sin. Life is short—temporal things appear very differently when one enters eternity!

If people only reflected more on God and on the joys of Heaven, the trials of life would be easier to bear and individuals would do whatever was necessary to get there. Christ said: "Lay up for yourselves treasures in Heaven, where neither rust nor moth consumes, nor thieves break in and steal. For where thy treasure is, there also will thy heart be."[414] St. Therese of Lisieux said, "Let us go forward in peace, our eyes upon Heaven, the only one goal of our labors."[415]

Jesus was transfigured and rose from the dead with a glorified body to remind us of *the resurrection of the body*. The glorified body, the good receive after the Last Judgment will enjoy perfect happiness forever in Heaven. The immortalized body[416] of unrepentant sinners will reside eternally in Hell.

Death

Death naturally occurs when the soul separates from the body. St. Anselm says no one can escape death, but its hour is uncertain. Since death brings about one's entrance into eternity, it is better to prepare spiritually for that event than fear it.

There are four possible destinations for the soul. The soul of a person who was baptized, died in the state of sanctifying grace and made up for the temporal punishment due to sin by prayer and good works, enters *Heaven*. Those who have not atoned for the temporal punishment of their venial sins are cleansed in the fires of *Purgatory* until this purification process is completed. There they also endure the pain of loss by their temporary separation from God.

The souls of unbaptized infants and the unbaptized who die before attaining the use of reason go to a place of earthly happiness similar to the Garden of Paradise called *Limbo*. They are perfectly content there, but will never see God.

---

[413] Matthew 16, 16.
[414] Matthew 6, 20-21.
[415] Holy card printed by the Office Central de Lisieux.
[416] A body that will never die.

Those who die in unrepentant mortal sin will be cast into the eternal flames of *Hell* where there is no relief, no hope and where they will endure sufferings that will never end.

Judging Others

It is not the right of humans to judge others and determine who is saved and who is not. Christ addressed the issue at the Sermon on the Mount.

> Do not judge, that you may not be judged. For with what judgment you judge, you shall be judged and with what measure you measure, it shall be measured to you.[417]

The *Dies Irae* Sequence of the Mass of the Dead elucidates this point when it ponders the thought that if at the Last Judgment the just will hardly be secure, what will become of me?

Judgment

Jesus reserves judgment of each individual to Himself. This will occur immediately after death at the site of a person's passing and is called the *Particular Judgment*. There is no appeal from this final sentence as time abruptly ends for that individual and eternity begins.

Since this life is a testing ground, a person who has attained the use of reason either uses the time given to prove his or her fidelity to God or misuses it by stubbornly rejecting God and His laws. One cannot remain neutral.

As a scuba diver needs special equipment to survive and function underwater, so those who enter the next life need an immortalized body. It will either enjoy the everlasting happiness of Heaven, the joys of Limbo or endure the unending fires of Hell.

Everyone will receive an immortalized body at the End of the World at the *Last Judgment (General Judgment)*. The day of reckoning will be held at the Valley of Josaphat[418] outside Jerusalem. There all the good and evil performed by each person on earth will be manifested to everyone who has ever lived. Theologians believe, all sins confessed in the Sacrament of Penance will not be included since God has already pardoned them.

Heaven

Heaven is a place of eternal happiness where the Blessed Trinity: Father, Son and Holy Ghost dwell with the Blessed Virgin Mary, angels and saints. The Apostles' Creed ends with the words *...and life everlasting. Amen.* Even though most Catholics have recited these words hundreds of times, most seldom reflect on their meaning.

The Catechism of the Council of Trent teaches that these words refer to the enjoyment of perfect happiness.[419] Scripture says the wonders of Heaven are beyond human comprehension:

> Eye has not seen nor ear heard, nor has it entered the heart of man, what things God has prepared for those who love Him.[420] ...I saw a great multitude which no man could number, out of all nations and tribes and peoples and tongues, standing before the throne...[421]

Those who save their immortal souls after death will hear from the lips of Christ the words:

> Come, blessed of my Father, take possession of the kingdom prepared for you from the foundation of the world.[422]

---

[417] Matthew 7, 1.
[418] The Hebrew translation of Josaphat is: *Jehovah judges.*
[419] pp. 132-133.
[420] 1 Corinthians 2, 9.
[421] Apocalypse 7, 9.
[422] St. Matthew 25, 34.

The *Catechism of the Council of Trent* teaches:

> The happiness of eternal life is, as defined by the Fathers, *an exemption from evil, and an enjoyment of all good.*[423] [It defines the Beatific Vision:] For the blessed always see God present and by this greatest and most exalted of gifts, being made *partaker of the divine nature,*[424] they enjoy true and solid happiness.[425]

There each person will be rewarded for a life of virtue and all will be immersed in God who is the infinite source of goodness. The saints in Heaven see God face to face in the *beatific vision* and are drawn to Him as iron is to a magnet. It is a happiness that will never end.

In Heaven, all trials, sufferings, temptations overcome, tears shed for others or in sorrow for sin, charitable actions, fidelity to God, and perseverance will be rewarded beyond measure. There will be no sadness, remorse or tediousness.

St. John in the Apocalypse[426] describes Heaven where:

> God will wipe away every tear from their eyes. And death shall be no more, neither mourning, nor crying, nor pain any more for the former things have passed away.

There is no jealousy in Heaven because everyone there is united to God. Each saint is perfectly happy, yet rewarded according to merits gained on earth. Heaven, don't miss it for the world.[427]

Saints and spiritual writers compare individuals in Heaven to vessels, some larger, some smaller. Each is filled with happiness to the brim, yet some have a greater capacity than others due to additional merits earned while on earth.

The eyes will behold God, Mary, angels, and saints; the ears, celestial music, and the heart will be filled to overflowing with perfect happiness. "But the just shall live for evermore ...they receive a kingdom of glory and a crown of beauty at the hand of the Lord."[428]

Purgatory

Purgatory is a temporary place of punishment and purgation where souls are purified and released once they have atoned for their sins. They can be assisted by the prayers of the faithful and by indulgences gained on their behalf. The Book of Machabees says "It is therefore a holy and wholesome thought to pray for the dead, that they may be loosed from sins."[429] Those in Purgatory, once they reach Heaven, will ask God to bless those who assisted them.

The Faithful Departed in Purgatory will have many regrets since much of their suffering could have been avoided. Many will lament that they didn't attend Mass more frequently or say their prayers daily, nor frequented the Sacraments of Penance and Holy Eucharist which could have merited them many graces and repaired for their sins.

Others will wish they had practiced charity when the opportunity arose and forgiven injuries. All will sadly realize they will not be released until full restitution is made for their sins.

---

[423] p. 135, Chrysost., *Ep. I ad Theod. lapsum*; Aug., *De Civitate Dei*, lib. xxii. cap. 30.
[424] 2 Peter 1, 4.
[425] p. 137.
[426] Chapter 21, Verse 4.
[427] A bumper sticker message.
[428] Wisdom 5, 16-17.
[429] 2 Machabees 12, 46.

Hell

Hell is a place of unending suffering and eternal separation from God. Our Lord will say to the damned at their judgment, "Depart from Me, accursed ones, into the everlasting fire which was prepared for the devil and his angels."[430] St. Alphonsus says the worst pain in Hell is eternal separation from God. Hell is mentioned 427 times in Scripture.

Those confined in this oven of fire will forever mourn their plight, yet nothing can be done to change it. The time of trial has passed.

Condemned to a pool of eternal fire, devils and the damned lament how easy it would have been for them to obey God's commands and merit Heaven. Demons and the lost will replay in their minds all that God had done for them. They realize that their rebellion against Him was base ingratitude and understand their punishment is just.

Damned human beings will realize they have spurned Jesus' Sufferings and Death on the Cross by a life of selfishness and sin. Even though He opened the Gates of Heaven for others, they will be forever separated from His love and confined in eternal flames.

Sadly, no one cares or can help another in Hell. The lost will never experience love. All suffer uselessly. What a waste! The damned could have been angels and saints in Heaven if they chose to lead a good life. Their sad plight could have been prevented by prayer.

In Hell, the devils torment the damned while lost souls curse the demons who tempted them. The terrible confinement in Hell worsens each time another enters. St. Alphonsus teaches the damned remain eternally fixed in the position in which they entered.

An Empty Existence

Life without God is personified in the empty obituary of an atheist:

> There will be no viewing or visitation. Cremation and burial took place without services ...an avowed atheist and maven of good beer, fine wine, choice bourbon, and single malt scotch whiskey requested that those desiring to remember and commemorate his life raise a glass and have a drink to his memory.[431]

Dying Unprepared

Ruthless Cesare Borgia led an evil life and was feared by all. He rarely considered the possibility of death and acted as though he would live forever.

Death came suddenly and quickly in the heat of battle. The last words from his mouth were a lament that he was unprepared to die. This was not a good way to enter eternity.

Jesus warned His followers:

> Do not love the world, or the things that are in the world. If anyone loves the world, the love of the Father is not in him; because all that is in the world is the lust of the flesh, and the lust of the eyes and the pride of life; which is not of the Father, but from the world. And the world with its lust is passing away, but he who does the will of God abides forever. [432]

Each person is only given one life. Live it in a manner pleasing to God.

---

[430] Matthew 25, 41.
[431] *Observer and Eccentric*, Livonia, Michigan, September 16, 2010, p. B6.
[432] 1 John 2, 15.

Chapter Forty-One

Sacramentals

The *Baltimore Catechism* calls sacramentals holy things or actions, the Church uses to obtain spiritual and temporal favors from God.[433] Therefore, blessed objects should be treated with respect.

Author Philip Weller[434] describes the close relationship that exists between sacraments and sacramentals, noting that sacramentals both prepare one for receiving the sacraments, and perpetuate the work of the sacraments. The Church, not Christ, instituted sacramentals.

Holy water, Epiphany water, Easter water, the sprinkling with holy water during High Mass and the blessing of babies and children somewhat resemble **Baptism**.

The Apostolic Blessing and other blessings, and exorcisms compliment the Sacrament of **Penance**.

Blessings of bread, wine, candles, crucifixes, sacred images, liturgical vestments, churches, sacred vessels, and altars remind one of the Mass, and the Sacraments of **Holy Orders** and the **Holy Eucharist**.

The blessings of schools, libraries, church bells and printing presses demonstrate how the graces of **Confirmation** continue to affect souls.

Blessings of expectant mothers, of a mother after the birth of a child, of fields, grain mills, animals, homes, fruit, produce and other foods show the solicitous care of the Church over couples and families after they have received the Sacrament of **Matrimony**.

Ceremonies blessing the sick and elderly, ambulances, hospitals, cemeteries, and graves manifest the respect for the dying and the dead seen in the rite of **Extreme Unction**.

Blessings and Blessed Items

A **constitutive blessing** causes an object to be sacred and set apart for religious purposes only. The blessing remains until the object is destroyed, sold or is no longer recognizable.[435] Therefore, irreparable statues are not to be tossed in the trash, but are to be burned and buried or broken into pieces and buried. Old vestments and old scapulars are to be burned and the ashes are buried. Ashes used for Ash Wednesday come from old palms that have been burned.

By means of an **invocative blessing** a priest asks God to bless the individual (parishioner, benefactor, sick person, animal), place (church, home, school, convent, factory) or object (car, airplane, helicopter). The blessing petitions God to watch over the individual and protect one from harm. Items blessed in this fashion do not have to be disposed of in a special manner.

Blessings that are performed in a church,[436] require a priest or bishop to be clothed in cassock (or religious habit), surplice and stole[437] and the items sprinkled with holy water. Objects that have been blessed do not lose their blessing if they are repaired, replated or given away.

---

[433] See Fr. Connell, #3, p. 312.
[434] See the Introduction to his book *The Roman Ritual: Part III Blessings*, p. xii.
[435] This would occur if a wooden altar was destroyed in a fire, or cut up into boards so that it was no longer an altar.
[436] The blessing of Rosaries does not require surplice, stole or holy water, although they may be used.
[437] Customarily the color of the day is used unless a white, red or violet stole is required by the rubrics.

The words of the rite for a blessing must be read exactly from the *Rituale Romanum,* making distinctions for singular (one) or plural (many). There are often vernacular translations of the prayers so bystanders can better understand what the priest is saying.

Scapulars

Scapulars are composed of two small rectangular pieces of blessed woolen cloth of the same color and fabric of material found on the habits or scapulars of various Religious Orders and are attached by two cords and worn over the shoulders. Laity and clergy who wear the scapular must be enrolled in order to gain the indulgences attached to them.

Our Lady gave the Brown Scapular of Our Lady of Mt. Carmel to Carmelite St. Simon Stock in Aylesford, England on July 16, 1251. This highly indulgenced sacramental comes with Mary's promise that whoever dies piously wearing the scapular will not suffer eternal fire. Individuals wearing the scapular must lead a good life in order to validate the promise. Pope Pius XII called the Brown Scapular a sign of consecration to Mary.

My twin brother, Fr. Dominic Radecki and I were amazed when a neighbor told us he was unhurt when he was shot during the Vietnam War since his Brown Scapular stopped the bullet. His devout mother faithfully prayed the Rosary daily for his safe return.

The Five-Way Scapular includes the Red Scapular of the Passion, the Brown Scapular (Carmelites), the Black Scapular of Our Lady of Sorrows (Servites), the Blue Scapular of the Immaculate Conception, and the White Scapular of the Blessed Trinity (Trinitarians).

In 1840, Mary gave the Green Scapular to a Daughter of Charity, Sr. Justine Bisqueyburu. It is used primarily for conversions and may be given to non-Catholics. The person giving or receiving the Green Scapular is requested to say daily: Immaculate Heart of Mary, pray for us now and at the hour of our death.

Wearing a scapular is a visible reminder to dress modestly and allows the person to share in the prayers and good works of the Religious Orders the scapular represents.

Blessed Medals

Medals with stamped images of Christ, Our Lady, saints, or angels are sacramentals that are often worn around the neck suspended by a chain or cord. The *St. Benedict Medal* and the *Miraculous Medal* (Medal of the Immaculate Conception) are the most highly indulgenced. Both are very powerful as a means of protection against the devil.

Chapter Forty-Two

Prayer

The *Baltimore Catechism* defines prayer as raising one's mind and heart to God. In simple terms, prayer is talking to God. By having daily communication and a loving conversation with God through prayer, the soul grows in grace and develops a closer union with Him.

The four ends of prayer are:

adoration	loving and honoring God
petition	asking God for assistance and favors
reparation	asking pardon of God
thanksgiving	thanking God for His favors and blessings

God always hears prayers, but doesn't give people what they want, but what is best for the individual at the time since He knows certain things may not be good for them.

Focus

St. Alphonsus says to persevere in prayer: pray daily with confidence and reverent devotion. God is more apt to hear one's prayer if the person is fervent and perseveringly asks for help.

"Before prayer, prepare thy soul."[438] Pause and briefly entrust all spiritual and material needs to His care. Focus on what you are saying and look at sacred pictures if it helps. Distractions are often caused either by the devil or by not preparing properly.

If thoughts of family, cares or material needs arise during prayer, banish them, unless there is an emergency, and return to prayer, asking God for assistance. St. Francis de Sales said that many times God Himself resolved difficulties as he prayed.

The spirit of prayer should become like second nature and pervade one's life, for Our Lord said, "we ought always to pray..."[439] Saints call this living in the presence of God.

Effects of Prayer

Prayer keeps a person's eyes on Heaven and helps one endure the difficulties in life. Temptations are overcome or banished by turning to God for assistance. Prayer with childlike confidence helps individuals realize that God cares and will assist, especially when asked.

Mental Prayer

Meditation is mental prayer that leads to closer union with God. It helps one focus on God's love, the lives of Jesus and Mary and the salvation of one's soul. The Catholic Church opposes transcendental meditation since it has Buddhist and Hindu roots and is self-absorbing.

The Stations of the Cross

The practice of the Stations of the Cross recalls Jesus' Passion and Death. Mary used to traverse the Way of the Cross in Jerusalem to revere the places where Christ suffered to repair for the sins of the world. Many imitated her actions and some even traveled to the Holy Land.

Due to the difficulty and danger of traveling to the Holy Land, popes granted indulgences to the Faithful who moved from station to station in church to imitate the actions of Our Lord and recall the events that occurred on Good Friday. When prayed in common, it suffices that the leader walks from station to station.

---

[438] Ecclesiasticus 18, 23.
[439] Luke 18, 1.

The Most Holy Rosary

Our Lady gave St. Dominic the Fifteen Mystery Rosary in 1214. This highly indulgenced devotion combines **vocal prayer**—the recitation of the Apostles' Creed, Our Father, Hail Mary, Glory Be, and the Fatima Prayer[440] with **mental prayer**—meditation on the holy lives of Jesus and Mary. It is customary for Catholics to pray five decades daily, preferably as a family.

Pope Pius XII wrote in the Encyclical[441] *Ingruentium Malorum*:

> It is above all in the bosom of the family that we desire the custom of the holy Rosary to be everywhere adopted, religiously preserved and evermore intensely practiced. What a sweet sight, most pleasing to God, when the Christian home resounds with the repetition of the praises in honor of the August Queen of Heaven.

The Fifteen Mysteries of the Rosary

The Joyful Mysteries

The Annunciation	Angel Gabriel asks Mary to be the Mother of the Messias
The Visitation	Mary visits her cousin St. Elizabeth
The Nativity	Jesus is born in Bethlehem
The Presentation	Our Lady and St. Joseph present Jesus in the Temple
The Finding in the Temple	Mary and St. Joseph find Christ in Jerusalem

The Sorrowful Mysteries

The Agony in the Garden	Jesus in the Garden of Gethsemane
The Scourging at the Pillar	Our Lord suffers for the sins of the world
The Crowning with Thorns	Christ is mocked by the Roman Soldiers
The Carrying of the Cross	Jesus journeys to Mt. Calvary
The Crucifixion	Our Redeemer dies on the Cross

The Glorious Mysteries

The Resurrection	Jesus rises from the dead
The Ascension	Our Lord ascends into Heaven
The Descent of the Holy Ghost	Mary and the Apostles receive the Holy Ghost
The Assumption	Our Lady is taken to Heaven
The Coronation	Mary is crowned Queen of Heaven and Earth

Pope St. Pius X said: "Of all prayers, the Rosary is the most beautiful and the richest in graces; of all, it is one which is most pleasing to Mary, the Virgin Most Holy."[442]

Joyful Mysteries are prayed on Mondays, Thursdays and on the Sundays of Advent, Christmas, Epiphany, and Septuagesima.

Sorrowful Mysteries are prayed on Tuesdays, Fridays and on Sundays during Lent.

Glorious Mysteries are prayed on Wednesdays, Saturdays and on all remaining Sundays.

---

[440] Our Lady of Fatima requested that the following prayer be recited after each decade: O my Jesus, forgive our sins. Save us from the fires of Hell. Lead all souls to Heaven, especially those who have most need of Thy mercy.
[441] September 15, 1951.
[442] Philip O'Reilley, *1000 Questions and Answers on Catholicism*, p. 143.

Chapter Forty-Three
Using Time Well

There is only one thing on earth that you can have, make, buy, lose, find, save, or waste. You can buy it, but it's not for sale, you can lose it, but few find it. It can be saved or wasted. Although only a concept, it is very real. It is composed of only four letters, yet touches eternity. The use of it will determine one's final abode. What is it? Time.

God is beyond time because He is eternal.

Make time for prayer. Find time to daily get closer to God.

Arrange time to teach your children the faith.

Get to Mass on time; it is the most grace-filled time of the day.

Talk to Jesus during the time He abides in your heart at Holy Communion.

Confession and Holy Communion need to be more frequent than just during Easter time.

Practice charity and avoid spending extra time in Purgatory.

Set aside quality time for your spouse and family. Take time to recharge.

Don't waste time on long phone calls, texting or surfing the Internet.

When time ends, where will you spend eternity?

Although many wonder what is required to become a saint and get to Heaven, it simply comes down to using time properly. Everyone is allotted only a certain period of time. Eternity begins once the hourglass runs out.

Even though many think time is endless, no one can be sure of being alive tomorrow. The end of the world comes for each individual when God calls. Hopefully, all of one's sins will have been pardoned and atonement made before entering eternity.

Those who lead a life of sin and selfishness go to judgment devoid of merits and deserving of punishment. Unforgiven mortal sin will be the cause of the damnation of millions.

God rewards those who remain faithful to Him on earth with an eternity of happiness. Prayers, good works, Masses attended, sacraments received, Rosaries prayed, temptations overcome, and virtues practiced are spiritual treasures that merit reward. Spend time well in order to persevere and die in God's grace. While taking time for others, never neglect oneself.

St. John Chrysostom says, 'Whoever arms himself with prayer will not sin...' and that prayer 'is a powerful means of warding off the attacks of the devil, and affords us protection against all dangers.' St. Ephrem writes: 'It preserves moderation, represses anger, checks pride and envy, quiets feelings of revenge, draws down the Holy Ghost upon the soul and raises man to Heaven.'[443] St. Alphonsus Liguori said:

> A person who prays will certainly be saved, but a person who does not pray will certainly be lost. All who have been saved, were saved through prayer. All who have been lost were lost through their neglect of prayer.[444]

[443] Very Rev. Charles Callan, OP, *Illustrations for Sermons and Instructions*, p. 185.
[444] Benedictine Convent of Perpetual Adoration, Clyde, Missouri, *Prayer: the Great Means of Grace*, p. 7-8.

Daily Prayers

Catholics should daily recite the Morning Offering on rising to offer the day to God. Before retiring, it is customary to say the Angel of God prayer, make a short examination of conscience and recite the Act of Contrition.

In order to persevere in the grace of God in these turbulent times, it is almost essential to pray five decades of the Rosary daily. The Holy Sacrifice of the Mass is the greatest prayer, and the time after reception of Holy Communion, the most precious of one's life.

St. Therese of Lisieux said prayer should not be complicated, nor like a mathematical formula. There is a big difference between devotion and devotions. The Book of Proverbs beautifully summarizes prayer in the words: "I love them that love Me: and they that in the morning early watch for Me, shall find Me."[445]

The Promises of Christ

The prayer, Hail Holy Queen ends with a versicle and response:

Pray for us, O holy Mother of God.   That we may be made worthy of the promises of Christ.

What are the promises of Christ? These can be found in the Gospels. Below are some of them.

- "He who believes and is baptized shall be saved."[446]

- "Blessed are those who have not seen and yet have believed."[447]

- "I am with you all days, even unto the consummation of the world."[448]

- "If anyone love Me, he will keep My word, and My Father will love him, and We will come to him and make Our abode with him."[449]

- "Come to Me, all you who labor and are burdened and I will give you rest."[450]

- "...as long as you did it for one of these, the least of my brethren, you did it for Me."[451]

- "Ask, and it shall be given you; seek, and you shall find; knock, and it shall be opened to you."[452]

- "...everyone who acknowledges Me before men, I will acknowledge before my Father in Heaven."[453]

- "He who eats My Flesh and drinks My Blood has life everlasting and I will raise him up on the last day."[454]

- "Not everyone who says to me, 'Lord, Lord' shall enter the kingdom of Heaven; but he who does the will of my Father in Heaven shall enter the kingdom of Heaven."[455]

---

[445] Chapter 8, Verse 17.
[446] Mark 16, 16.
[447] John 20, 29.
[448] Matthew 28, 20.
[449] John 14, 23.
[450] Matthew 11, 28.
[451] Matthew 25, 40.
[452] John 16, 24.
[453] Matthew 10, 32.
[454] John 6, 55.
[455] Matthew 7, 21.

Questions

Chapter 1 Proofs for the Existence of God

1. What is meant by the words *First Cause*?
2. How do cause and effect prove the existence of God?
3. How does order in the universe prove there must be a God?
4. Explain conscience.
5. Is God all-just? Explain.

Chapter 2 Atheistic Evolution / The Big Bang Theory

1. Who was Pierre Laplace?
2. Is there any tangible proof for Darwin's theory of evolution?
3. What is the Second Law of Thermodynamics?
4. Could God have started the world with a Big Bang? Explain.
5. Why do true scientists know a Creator made the world?

Chapter 3 The Blessed Trinity

1. Who is God?
2. Name the Three Divine Persons.
3. Name two physical objects that demonstrate three in one.
4. What occurred at Jesus' Baptism?
5. What obligation does a person have to God?

Chapter 4 Erroneous Concepts of God

1. Define agnosticism.
2. Define atheism.
3. Define materialism.
4. Define pantheism.
5. Why is reincarnation unreasonable?

Chapter 5 Unjustly Blaming God for Difficulties

1. What are physical evils?
2. Does God directly will or merely permit evil?
3. Why does God allow suffering and trials in life?
4. Can these be meritorious?
5. What is Divine Providence?

Chapter 6 Angels

1. Why did God create angels and humans?
2. Name four satanic practices that endanger the soul.
3. What means can be used to combat devils?
4. Name three major archangels.
5. Name three biblical events at which angels were present.

Chapter 7 Humans

1. Why did God create humans?
2. Name the three types of gifts God gave Adam and Eve.
3. Who did Adam blame after eating the forbidden fruit? Who did Eve blame?
4. Name four punishments God gave Adam and Eve and their offspring.
5. What was the greatest gift Adam and Eve lost at the Fall?

Chapter 8 The Redeemer

1. What does the word *Incarnation* mean?
2. Why did the Redeemer have to be God-man?
3. Name two of the effects of the Redemption.
4. Name three of Christ's miracles.
5. What artifact proves the Passion and Resurrection of Christ?

Chapter 9 The Blessed Virgin Mary

1. Where is the first scriptural reference to Mary?
2. Which prophet predicted that the Messias would be born of a virgin?
3. What do the words *Immaculate Conception* mean?
4. Why is Mary rightly called Mother of God?
5. Why is Mary called co-Redemptrix?

Chapter 10 Grace

1. Why is grace necessary for salvation?
2. What is actual grace?
3. What is sanctifying grace?
4. Does God give everyone sufficient grace to be saved? Explain.
5. How does one fall from grace?

Chapter 11 Faith

1. Why is faith the foundation of the other virtues?
2. Which saint said that faith without works is dead?
3. How does supernatural faith affect a person's life?
4. Describe the difference between pleasure and happiness.
5. Explain peace of soul.

Chapter 12 Hope

1. What is the virtue of hope?
2. Name three books from the Old Testament that inspire one to have hope.
3. Name three things needed for a good foundation of a marriage.
4. What are presumption and despair?
5. When is the virtue of hope most necessary?

Chapter 13 Charity

1. What is the virtue of charity?
2. Give an example of Christian charity.
3. What is the difference between will and emotion?
4. What is the difference between the corporal and spiritual works of mercy?
5. Name the four cardinal virtues.

Chapter 14 Temptation

1. Is temptation a sin?
2. How does a person overcome temptation?
3. What is full consent?
4. What is partial consent?
5. Name three holy men that fell in the Old Testament.

Chapter 15 Sin

1. Name four ways a person can sin.
2. Why are venial sins not to be taken lightly?
3. Why is mortal sin deadly?
4. Name the Seven Capital Sins.
5. What three conditions are necessary for a sin to be mortal?

Chapter 16 The First Commandment

1. What is the First Commandment?
2. Why are Catholics forbidden to actively participate in non-Catholic religious ceremonies?
3. Name four popes who condemned *communicatio in sacris*.
4. Why is the use of Ouija Boards sinful?
5. Describe the difference between a heretic and an apostate.

Chapter 17 The Third Commandment

1. Why is Mass attendance obligatory on Sundays and Holy Days?
2. Name two things forbidden by the Third Commandment.
3. Name the three essential elements of the Mass.
4. What are Rogation Days and Ember Days?
5. What three languages are used in the Tridentine Latin Mass?

Chapter 18 The Second Commandment

1. Why is it wrong to use the name of God in surprise and anger?
2. Name a vow commonly taken today.
3. Why is it wrong to say "I swear to God" unnecessarily?
4. Why is perjury a mortal sin?
5. How can a person stop the habit of using God's name in vain?

Chapter 19 The Fourth Commandment

1. Why must children show respect for their parents?
2. How does one show love for parents?
3. Why is it important to listen to those in authority?
4. Why is disobedience wrong?
5. Is it wrong to delay in obeying?

Chapter 20 The Fifth Commandment

1. How can sarcasm become sinful?
2. Is abortion a mortal sin? Why?
3. How does a person repair the reputation of another?
4. Why is it a mortal sin to drive under the influence?
5. Why is drug abuse wrong?

Chapter 21 The Eighth Commandment

1. Why is honesty important for a person's character?
2. What is culpable negligence?
3. Why is "white lie" a contradiction of terms?
4. What is rash judgment?
5. Why are slander and detraction so detestable to God?

Chapter 22 The Sixth and Ninth Commandments

1. How can a person preserve purity?
2. What did Christ mean when He said, "the clean of heart shall see God?"
3. Why did Jesus call the eyes "the windows of the soul?"
4. Why must occasions of sin be avoided?
5. Why is purity like a priceless diamond?

Chapter 23 The Seventh and Tenth Commandments

1. Why did God command all to respect the property of others?
2. Why should people be content with necessities?
3. How does one practice justice in the workplace?
4. What did St. Augustine say about restitution?
5. Will material goods ever make anyone perfectly happy?

Chapter 24 What Makes a Sin Mortal?

1. Most mortal sins offend against what three virtues?
2. What does the word *voluntary* mean?
3. What causes the matter of sin to be grave?
4. How do sins of thought become serious?
5. Why is the omission of the Easter duty a serious sin?

Chapter 25 Spiritual Blindness

1. How does one become spiritually blind?
2. What are the consequences of spiritual blindness?
3. How can it be overcome?
4. How does one who has fallen return to God?
5. How did God punish Nebuchadnezzar?

Chapter 26 Saints

1. Why do Catholics use statues and sacred images?
2. What non-religious images are commonly seen in cities today?
3. Why are the bodies of the departed to be buried, not cremated?
4. Explain the difference between latria, hyperdulia and dulia.
5. What are relics and why are they revered?

Chapter 27 The Seven Sacraments

1. Why did Christ institute the Seven Sacraments?
2. What are the four essential elements for each sacrament?
3. Explain *ex opere operato*.
4. Explain *ex opere operantis*.
5. What three oils are used in the sacraments?

Chapter 28 Baptism

1. Name the five effects of Baptism.
2. What are baptismal vows?
3. Why is Baptism necessary for salvation?
4. What does the lighted candle used during the ceremony represent?
5. What is conditional Baptism?

Chapter 29 Penance

1. When did the Apostles receive the power to forgive sin?
2. Why did Christ institute the Sacrament of Penance?
3. What is meant by the Confessional Seal?
4. What is an Examination of Conscience?
5. What is a Firm Purpose of Amendment?

Chapter 30 The Holy Eucharist

1. What is the Holy Eucharist?
2. What is the Communion Fast?
3. What is the Easter Duty?
4. Why should one make a thanksgiving after Holy Communion?
5. What three requirements are necessary to receive the Holy Eucharist?

Chapter 31 Confirmation

1. How did Pentecost transform the Apostles?
2. What are the four effects of Confirmation?
3. Name the Seven Gifts of the Holy Ghost.
4. Name the Twelve Fruits of the Holy Ghost.
5. Why is Confirmation important today?

Chapter 32 Matrimony

1. Who is the minister for the Sacrament of Matrimony?
2. What are the Laws of the Church concerning marriage?
3. What is the primary purpose of marriage?
4. What is the secondary purpose of marriage?
5. What are the two essential properties of marriage?

Chapter 33 Holy Orders

1. What is priestly celibacy?
2. What is Apostolic Succession?
3. Who possesses the fullness of the priesthood?
4. What are the main duties of priests and bishops?
5. Why is the priesthood the lifeblood of the Church?

Chapter 34 Extreme Unction

1. Should a person wait until immediately before death to receive Extreme Unction?
2. What are the effects of this sacrament?
3. What are the Last Sacraments?
4. What parts of the body are anointed during Extreme Unction?
5. What is Holy Viaticum and what do the Latin words mean?

Chapter 35 The Catholic Church

1. What do the three rings of the papal tiara represent?
2. Who is the Head of the Catholic Church?
3. What is papal infallibility?
4. What is indefectibility?
5. What is an *interregnum*?

Chapter 36 The Deposit of Faith

1. What is the Deposit of Faith?
2. What was the ancient Greek Old Testament called?
3. What is an ancient codex of Scripture?
4. Which saint wrote the Latin Vulgate Bible?
5. What is Apostolic Tradition?

Chapter 37 The Four Marks of the Church

1. Explain the unity of the Church.
2. Explain the holiness of the Church.
3. Explain the catholicity of the Church.
4. Explain the apostolicity of the Church.
5. Why did Jesus develop a visible Church?

Chapter 38 The Laws of Fast and Abstinence

1. Why do Catholics fast during the 40 days of Lent?
2. Who is bound to the laws of fast?
3. Who is bound to the laws of abstinence?
4. What foods must one avoid on days of abstinence?
5. Who is dispensed from fasting?

Chapter 39 Indulgences

1. What is a partial indulgence?
2. What is a plenary indulgence?
3. What are the requirements for gaining a plenary indulgence?
4. Why is it important to gain indulgences?
5. Why is it important to vocalize prayer?

Chapter 40 Life, Death, Judgment, Heaven, Hell

1. What is meant by the resurrection of the body?
2. Is death something to be feared?
3. What is the Particular Judgment?
4. How did St. Paul explain eternal happiness?
5. What causes a person to spend eternity in Hell?

Chapter 41 Sacramentals

1. What is a sacramental?
2. What is a constitutive blessing?
3. What is an invocative blessing?
4. Explain the importance of the Brown Scapular.
5. Which medals are very powerful against the devil?

Chapter 42 Prayer

1. What is the difference between vocal prayer and mental prayer?
2. Why must one pray daily?
3. Why should the Stations of the Cross be prayed during Lent?
4. Who began the practice of the Stations of the Cross?
5. Why is the Rosary so important?

Bibliography

Abbo, STL, JCD, John and Jerome Hannan, AM, LLB, STD, JCD. *The Sacred Canons: A Concise Presentation of the Current Disciplinary Norms of the Church: Vol. II*. St. Louis: B. Herder Book Co., 1952.

a' Kempis, Thomas. *My Imitation of Christ*. Brooklyn: Confraternity of the Precious Blood, 1982.

Alberione, SSP, STD, Very Rev. J. Translated by Hilda Calabro, MA. *Glories and Virtues of Mary*. Boston: St. Paul Editions, 1962.

Aquinas, St. Thomas. Translated by Fathers of the English Dominican Province. *Summa Theologica: Volume I*. New York: Benziger Brothers.

A Seminary Professor. *Exposition of Christian Doctrine: Part I Dogma*. Philadelphia: John Joseph McVey.

Attwater, Donald. *The Catholic Dictionary*. New York: Macmillan Company, 1953.

Barr, Stephen. *Modern Physics and Ancient Faith*. Notre Dame: University of Notre Dame Press, 2003.

Bierbaum, OFM, Fr. Athanasius. *Pusillum: Vol. I*. Chicago: Franciscan Herald Press, 1932.

———. *Pusillium. Vol. III*. Chicago: Franciscan Herald Press, 1945.

Birkhaeuser, Fr. J. *History of the Church from Its First Establishment to Our Own Times*. New York: Pustet, 1891.

Bouscaren, SJ, STD, LLB, T. *Canon Law Digest Volume III: Officially Published Documents Affecting the Code of Canon Law 1942-1953*. Milwaukee: Bruce Publishing Company, 1954.

Breviarium Romanum Pars Verna. Mechliniae: H. Dessain, 1955.

Bunson, Matthew. *Our Sunday Visitor's Encyclopedia of Catholic History*. Huntington, IN: Our Sunday Visitor Publishing Division, 1995.

Callan, OP, Very Rev. Charles. *Illustrations for Sermons and Instructions*. New York: Joseph Wagner, Inc., 1916.

Carey, MA, Rev. James. *The Sunday Gospels for Priest and People*. New York: P. J. Kenedy, 1935.

www.cdc.gov/STD/ Downloaded on 2/13/14 at 5:47 a.m.

Chapin, John. *Book of Catholic Quotations*. New York: Farrar, Stauss and Cudahy, 1956.

Chautard, OCR, Dom J. Translated by Rev. J. Moran. *The Soul of the Apostolate*. Techny, IL: Mission Press, 1941.

www.christiananswers.org/entry/Isaac_Newton Downloaded on 9/6/14 at 5:55 a.m.

christianity.about.com/od/faqhelpdesk/qt/whyeasterchange.htm Downloaded on 4/5/14 at 7:20 p.m.

Clarkson, SJ, John and John Edwards, SJ, Willam Kelly, SJ and John Welch, SJ. *The Church Teaches: Documents of the Church in English Translation*. St. Louis: Herder Book Co., 1955.

Confraternity of Christian Doctrine, Catholic Doctrine First Semester, Detroit, Michigan.

Connell, CSSR, STD, Fr. Francis. *Baltimore Catechism No. 3*. New York: Benziger Brothers, 1949.

———. *Outlines of Moral Theology*. Milwaukee: Bruce Publishing Company, 1953.

Conway, Rev. Bertrand. *The Question Box: Replies to Questions Received on Missions to Non-Catholics*. New York: Paulist, 1929.

Cruz, Joan Carroll. *The Incorruptibles*. Rockford: Tan Books and Publishers, 1977.

Davis, SJ, Henry. *Moral & Pastoral Theology (Summary)*. New York: Sheed & Ward, 1952.

De Aquino, Sanctus Thomas. *Summa Theologiae: II Prima Secundae*. Ottawa, Canada: Commissio Piana, 1953.

de Montfort, St. Louis Marie. Translated by Mary Barbour. *The Secret of the Rosary*. Bay Shore, NY: Montfort Publications, 1954.

Denzinger Henrici. *Enchiridion Symbolorum: Definitionem et Declarationum de Rebus Fidei et Morum*. Friburgi: Sumptibus Herder. 1952.

———. Translated by Roy Deferrari. *The Sources of Catholic Dogma*. St. Louis: B. Herder Book Co., 1957

142

Doheny, CSC, JUD, Msgr. William and Rev. Joseph Kelly, STD. *Papal Documents on Mary.* Milwaukee: Bruce Publishing Co., 1954.

drbo.org Downloaded on 10/21/13 at 6:15 a.m. and frequently throughout the composition of this book.

Drinkwater, Rev. F. *Catechism Stories: A Teacher's Aid Book: Part I The Creed.* London: Burns, Oates & Washbourne Ltd., 1939.

Ecker, DD, PhD, Rev. James. Translated by Rev. Patrick Cummins, OSB, DD and Rev. Lawrence Villing, OSB. *Bible Lessons.* St. Louis: B. Herder Book Co., 1918.

en.wikipedia.org/wiki/Albert_of_Mainz Downloaded on 5/8/14 at 8:45 p.m.

en.wikipedia.org/wiki/Codex_Ephraemi_Rescriptus Downloaded on 10/6/14 at 5:20 p.m.

en.wikipedia.org/wiki/Cult_of_Reason Downloaded on 12/28/13 at 6:15 a.m.

en.wikipedia.org/wiki/Cult_of_the_Supreme_Being Downloaded on 12/28/13 at 6:22 a.m.

en.wikipedia.org/wiki/Transmutation_of_species Downloaded on 3/8/15 at 10:50 p.m.

en.wikipedia.org/wiki/Yoga Downloaded on 11/26/13 at 10:10 a.m.

Fillion, SS, L. Translated by John Reville, SJ, PhD. *The Study of the Bible.* New York: P. J. Kenedy & Sons, 1926.

Gasparri, Peter Cardinal. Translated by Rev. Hugh Pope, OP, *The Catholic Catechism.* New York: P. J. Kenedy & Sons, 1932.

Glenn, PhD, STD, Rt. Rev. Msgr. Paul. *Apologetics.* St. Louis: B. Herder Book Co., 1931.

www.godandscience.org/apologetics/quotes.html#n02 Downloaded on 5/13/14 at 8:00 p.m.

Green, Michael and Greg Stewart. *M1 Abrams at War.* St. Paul: Zenith Press, 2005.

Goldstein, LL.D, David. *What Say You?* St. Paul: Radio Replies Press, 1945.

Griffith, Fr. Paul. *Priest's New Ritual.* New York: P. J. Kenedy & Sons, 1947.

Halligan, OP, Nicholas. *Administration of the Sacraments.* New York: Alba House, 1963.

Haydock, Fr. George. *Douay Rheims Holy Bible with Catholic Commentary.* Duarte, CA: Catholic Treasures, 2006.

Herbermann, PhD, LLD, Charles. *Catholic Encyclopedia: Vols. 1, 5, 6, 13, 15.* New York: The Encyclopedia Press, 1908.

history.hanover.edu/texts/trent/trentall.html Downloaded on 2/24/15 at 5:34 a.m.

Howe, Very Rev. Canon G. *Stories from the Catechist.* Rockford: Tan Books and Publishers, 1987.

Holy Bible. New York: P. J. Kenedy & Sons, 1950.

Holy Bible (Douay-Rheims Version) *Biblia Sacra* (juxta Vulgatum Clementinam). London: Baronius Press, 2008.

Hutchins, J. *Hubble Reveals Creation By An Awe-Inspiring Power.* Orlando: Imagination Publishing, 2012.

Jone, OFM, Rev. Heribert and Rev. Urban Adelman, OFM Cap, JCD. *Moral Theology.* Westminster, MD: The Newman Press, 1957.

Kinkead, Rev. Thomas. *Baltimore Catechism, No. 4,* New York: Benziger Brothers, 1921.

Krull, CPPS Rev. Vigilius. *Christian Denominations.* Cleveland: John Winterich, 1925.

MacLoughlin, Rev. James. *Catholic Faith in Outline: A Summary of Instruction A Guide for Preacher and Teacher.* Dublin: Cahill & Co. Ltd., 1955.

Markma, Ian. *Against Atheism: Why Dawkins, Hitchens, & Harris are Fundamentally Wrong.* West Sussex: Wiley-Blackwell, 2010.

Martinez, DD, Archbishop Luis. *Only Jesus.* St. Louis: B. Herder Book Co., 1962.

———. *Secrets of the Interior Life.* Manchester, NH: Sophia Institute Press, 2004.

———. *The Sanctifier.* Pauline Books & Media, 2004.

McAuliffe SJ, Clarence. *Sacramental Theology: A Textbook for Advanced Students.* Binghamton: Vail-Ballou Press, 1958.

McGovern, DD, Rev. James. *The Manual of the Catholic Church.* Chicago: Catholic Art and Publication Office, 1906.

Merz, Philip. *Thesaurus Biblicus* or *Handbook of Scripture Reference.* translated by Rev. Lambert. Waterloo: Observer Book Publication Company, 1880.

Missale Romanum. Editio IX Taurinensis juxta typicam, Marietta, 1957.

Nevins, MM Albert. *The Maryknoll Catholic Dictionary.* Wilkes Barre: Dimension Books, 1964.

news.yahoo.com/big-bang-breakthrough-team-allows-may-wrong-114835743.html?soc_src=

New Testament. Paterson, NJ: Confraternity of Christian Doctrine, 1941.

North, Eric. *Book of a Thousand Tongues.* London: United Bible Societies, 1939.

Observer and Eccentric. Livonia, Michigan, September 16, 2010.

Orchard, MA, Dom Bernard. Edited by Rev. Edmund Sutcliffe, SJ, MA, Rev. Reginald Fuller, DD, LSS, and Dom Ralph Russell, DD, MA. *A Catholic Commentary on Holy Scripture.* Edinburgh: Thomas Nelson & Sons, 1953.

O'Reilley, Philip. *1000 Questions and Answers on Catholicism.* New York: Guild Press, 1955.

Ott, Ludwig. *Fundamentals of Catholic Dogma.* Cork, Ireland: Mercier Press, 1952.

Raab, OFM, Fr. Clement. *Twenty Ecumenical Councils of the Catholic Church.* Westminster: Newman Press, 1959.

Radecki, CMRI Fr. Francisco and Fr. Dominic Radecki, CMRI. *Tumultuous Times: The 20 General Councils of the Catholic Church and Vatican II and Its Aftermath.* Ashland, OH: Bookmasters: 2004.

Ramstein, OFM, CONV. STM, JUD, Rev. Matthew. *A Manual of Canon Law.* Hoboken: Terminal Printing and Publishing Co., 1947.

Ripley, Canon Francis. *This is the Faith: A Complete Explanation of the Catholic Faith.* Rockford, IL: Tan, 2002.

Rumble, MSC Rev. Dr. Leslie and Rev. Charles Carty. *Radio Replies: Third Volume.* St. Paul: Radio Replies Press, 1942.

Parente, STD, PhD, JCB, Fr. Pascal. *Beyond Space.* Rockford, IL: Tan Books and Publishers, 1961.

Issued by Pope Pius V. Translated by John McHugh, OP and Charles Callan, OP. *Catechism of the Council of Trent.* Fort Collins, CO: Roman Catholic Books, 1923.

Parish Priests of the Chicago Archdiocese. *Instructions for Non-Catholics.* Reprinted as: *Lesson in the Catholic Faith.* Chicago, IL: United Book Service, 1954.

Pivarunas, CMRI Most Rev. Mark. *Baptism of Desire and of Blood.* Mater Dei Seminary.

Issued by Order of Pope St. Pius V. Translated by John McHugh, OP, STM, LITT.D. and Charles Callan, OP, STM, LITT.D. *Catechism of the Council of Trent.* Fort Collins, CO: Roman Catholic Books, 1923.

Pius IX, Pope. *Quanto Conficiamur Moerore.* August 10, 1863.

Pius X, Pope St. *Codex Juris Canonici.* Westminster: Newman Press, 1949.

Pius XII, Pope. *The Mystical Body of Christ.* New York: Paulist Press, 1943.

Pius XII, Pope. *Six Encyclicals of Pius XII.* Glen Rock, NJ: Paulist Press, 1943.

Pohle, PhD, DD, Rt. Rev. Msgr. Joseph. Edited by Arthur Preuss. *God: His Knowability, Essence and Attributes.* St. Louis: B. Herder Book Co., 1925.

———. *The Sacraments: Volume I.* New York: Vail-Ballou Press, Inc., 1915.

———. *The Sacraments: Volume IV.* St. Louis: B. Herder Book Co., 1917.

Prayer: the Great Means of Grace, Clyde, Missouri: Benedictine Convent of Perpetual Adoration, 1956.

144

Schmitz, John. *The Second Law of Life: Energy, Technology and the Future of Earth as We Know It.* What Einstein Thought About Thermodynamics, Press Release, July 12, 2009.

Schwartz, PhD, Gary and William Simon. *The G.O.D. Experiments: How Science is Discovering God in Everything Including Us.* New York: Atria, 2006.

science.howstuffworks.com/life/evolution/female-ancestor.htm Downloaded on 6/27/14 at 10:30 a.m.

Scott, SJ, LittD, Martin. *Things Catholics are Asked About.* New York: P. J. Kenedy & Sons, 1927.

Smith, DD, PhD, Canon George. *The Teaching of the Catholic Church, Vol. I.* New York: Macmillan, 1950.

——. *The Teaching of the Catholic Church, Vol. II.* New York: Macmillan, 1950.

Spirago, Rev. Francis. Edited by Rev. Francis Clarke, SJ. *The Catechism Explained: an Exhaustive Explanation of the Catholic Religion.* Rockford: Tan Books Inc. 1983.

St. Leonard of Port Maurice. *The Hidden Treasure: Holy Mass.* Fresno: Academy Library Guild, 1952.

Tanquerey, SS, DD, Very Rev. Adolfe. Translated by Msgr. John Byrnes. *Manual of Dogmatic Theology: Volume One.* Tournai, Belgium: Desclee, 1959.

——. Translated by Msgr. John Byrnes. *Manual of Dogmatic Theology: Volume One.* Tournai, Belgium: Desclee, 1959.

——. Translated by Msgr. John Byrnes. *Manual of Dogmatic Theology: Volume Two.* Tournai, Belgium: Desclee, 1959.

——. *Synopsis Theologiae Dogmaticae Fundamentis.* Tournai, Belgium: Desclée, 1937.

——. *The Spiritual Life: A Treatise on Ascetical and Mystical Theology.* Tournai, Belgium: Desclée & Co., 1930.

Third Council of Baltimore. *Baltimore Catechism.* Baltimore: Forgotten Books, 1956.

Toal, DD, T. *The Sunday Sermons of the Great Fathers: Vol. I.* Chicago: Henry Regnery, 1957.

——. *The Sunday Sermons of the Great Fathers: Vol. IV.* Chicago: Henry Regnery, 1963.

Traupman, PhD, John. *The Bantam New College Latin & English Dictionary.* New York: Bantam Books, 1966.

Van Noort, STD, Msgr. G. *Christ's Church: Vol II.* Westminster: Newman Press, 1957.

Von Keeper, Right Rev. Paul. *More Joy.* Thompsons, TX: Holy Cross Publications, 1914.

w2.vatican.va/content/leo-xiii/en/encyclicals/documents/hf_l-xiii_enc_09051897_divinum-illud-munus.html Downloaded on 2/14/15 at 4:00 p.m.

Weller, MM, Philip. *The Roman Ritual: Volume III The Blessings.* Milwaukee: Bruce Publishing Company, 1946.

Whitcomb, Paul. *The Catholic Church Has the Answer.* Los Angeles: Loyola Book Co., 1961.

Willis, SJ, John. *The Teachings of the Church Fathers.* San Francisco: Ignatius Press, 2002.

Woywod, OFM, LLB, Fr. Stanislaus. *A Practical Commentary on the Code of Canon Law.* New York: Joseph Wagner, 1952.

——. *A Practical Commentary on the Code of Canon Law: Vol. II.* New York: Joseph Wagner, 1945.

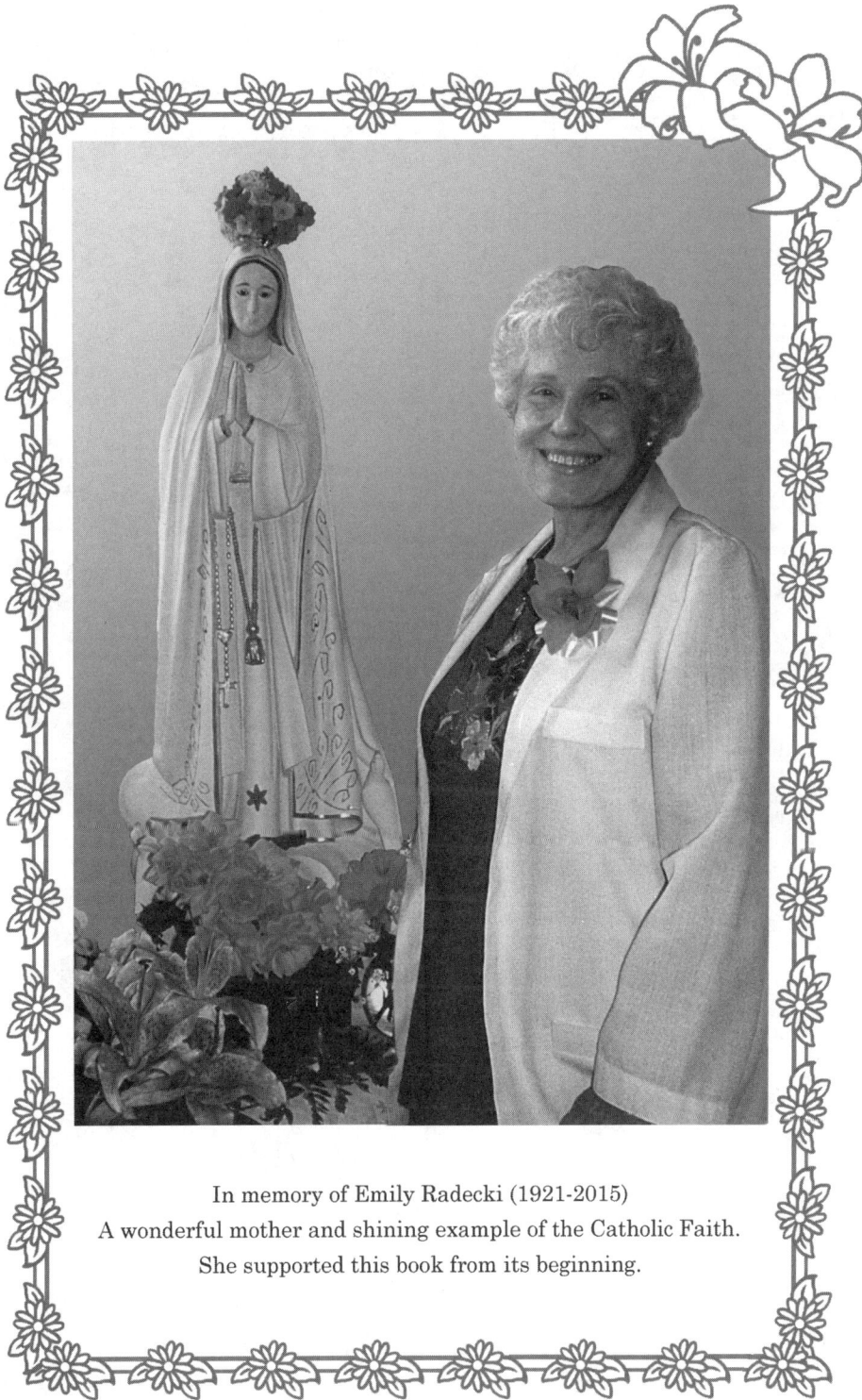

In memory of Emily Radecki (1921-2015)
A wonderful mother and shining example of the Catholic Faith.
She supported this book from its beginning.